TICKETS PLEASE!

A NOSTALGIC JOURNEY THROUGH RAILWAY STATION LIFE

A DAVID & CHARLES BOOK
David & Charles is an F+W Publications Inc. company

First published in the UK in 2006
This paperback edition first published in 2008

Text copyright © Paul Atterbury 2006, 2008

Distributed in North America by F+W Publications, Inc.
4700 East Galbraith Road Cincinnati, OH 45236
1-800-289-0963

A catalogue record for this book is available from the British Library.

ISBN-13 978-0-7153-2876-7 paperback
ISBN-10: 0-7153-2876-X paperback

Printed in China by SNP Leefung for David & Charles
Brunel House   Newton Abbot   Devon

Produced for David & Charles by
OutHouse Publishing
Shalbourne, Marlborough, Wiltshire SN8 3QJ

For OutHouse Publishing
Designer and Picture Researcher: Julian Holland
Editor and Project Manager: Sue Gordon

For David & Charles
Commissioning Editor: Mic Cady
Head of Design: Prudence Rogers
Design Assistant: Eleanor Stafford
Production Controller: Beverley Richardson

David & Charles books are available from all good bookshops;
alternatively you can contact our Orderline on (0)1626 334555 or write
to us at FREEPOST EX2 110, David & Charles Direct, Newton Abbot,
TQ12 4ZZ (no stamp required UK mainland).

Visit our website at www.davidandcharles.co.uk

▼ A modern view of Maiden Newton station on the line from Bristol
to Weymouth, set in the broad sweep of the Dorset hills.

TICKETS PLEASE!

A NOSTALGIC JOURNEY THROUGH RAILWAY STATION LIFE

Paul Atterbury

D&C
David and Charles

CONTENTS

Est. 766. 25,000. 2/28.   M 9801

L.N.E.R.

LUGGAGE.

From

To **MARYLEBONE** (LONDON)

SOUTHERN RAILWAY.
(7/24)
FROM WATERLOO TO
WEST PENNARD
787

INTRODUCTION

Even in the age of the car, the railway station, and all it represents, is at the heart of our culture. Yet, when the first passenger railways opened in the 1820s and 1830s stations barely existed. Not only did the Victorians create a national railway network, they also invented a new type of building, soon to be found in every town and city, and in many villages all over Britain. Style, scale and structure was infinitely varied but the station made its way into everyone's lives, whether they were off to school, the shops or work, on a day out or away on holiday. It became the setting for scenes of love and romance, war and conflict, drama and despair.

Since then, things have changed, and thousands of stations have disappeared as lines have closed. Yet, the station lives on in photographs and postcards, and in such ephemera as station signs and name boards, tickets and luggage labels. More importantly, stations live on in the imagination of those who remember them, or wish they did. This book celebrates stations past and present, and the life they saw, from busy city terminus to remote rural halt. It explores the impact of the station on our culture and history, and it marks the station as the greatest legacy of the railway age.

▲ Many closed stations have vanished, while others survive, hidden in the landscape. This overgrown platform is all that remains of Jedfoot, on the former Jedburgh branch in Scotland.

◄ Surviving on many stations are the cast-iron monograms of the companies that originally built the railways, as seen in this decorative Taff Vale Railway bracket.

► The humorous postcard is part of the history of the railway station, and the station experience. This Edwardian example features the universal fear of missing the last train.

▼ The railways made it possible to travel around the country in ways hitherto inconceivable. So stations, which were built entirely for the convenience of passengers, became an integral part of everyone's life – especially for going on holiday. Here, well-laden passengers disembark at Sandown, on the Isle of Wight in the 1950s.

The last Train.

THAT'S ME

STATION ARCHITECTURE

GOTHIC AND TUDOR

The great architectural debate of the 19th century was Gothic revival versus classical. Through the century the battle ranged widely and continuously, without clear winners or losers. The new Palace of Westminster was Gothic, the Foreign Office classical. The debate also divided the railway builders but they added a new regional angle with the north and north-west of England favouring the classical camp, while Gothic was more associated with the south of England, the Midlands, East Anglia, Wales and Scotland. Gothic was a very fashionable style indeed in the first part of the 19th century, and was at its peak from the 1830s to the 1870s. It was successful because it represented a sense of history, Christianity, wealth and extravagance, industrial and imperial success, and a strong element of patriotism. Gothic was above all else perceived as a suitably British style. To the Victorians, Gothic meant a number of things, including medievalism, Tudor, Jacobean and many aspects of the traditional vernacular, in fact anything that was not overtly classical. As a result, it could also incorporate European elements, notably Flemish, French, German and Italian. As a new building type, the railway station was a reflection of its age. It gloried in the stylistic confusion that Gothic and Tudor represented, but still saw it as eminently suitable for the new railway buildings of the modern age, combining history and permanence with new technology. It was also flexible, applicable alike to city termini and to country halts.

▲ There are many famous Gothic stations but few can compete with Bristol Temple Meads. Brunel was not a natural Goth, but his original 1840 terminus, to the left of the present station, flew the Gothic, or Tudor, flag. This set the pattern for the 1878 station, a glorious and extravagant structure with its famous central clock tower.

▼ This 1930s panoramic view of Gilbert Scott's majestic 1870s Midland Grand Hotel at St Pancras shows railway Gothic at its most imaginative and ambitious. With this building the Midland Railway put itself firmly on the map.

▲ This 1910 picture of Brading, on the Isle of Wight, shows the simplest possible use of Gothic, with arched windows added to a plain brick building.

▲ For country stations Brunel created a simple cottage style with Tudor and vernacular overtones, including hipped roofs or well-defined canopies. This drawing shows Twyford, in Berkshire, in the 1840s.

▲ The North Staffordshire Railway was adventurous in its architecture, favouring a decorative Tudor style that was the speciality of its chosen architect, Henry Hunt. Typical is Stone, built in 1849, a perfect small-scale exercise in the style, featuring careful symmetry, contrasting brick and stone, Flemish gables and tall, decorative chimneys. Recently restored, Stone is a fine memorial to local ambition and elegance.

▶ When completed in 1848, Brocklesby station, in Lincolnshire, was described as 'a very chaste erection in the pure Elizabethan style'. It was an ambitious building by the Manchester, Sheffield & Lincolnshire Railway and, although closed, survives.

CLASSICAL AND ITALIANATE

Dominant through the 18th century, the classical style had lost some of its appeal by the start of the railway age, partly because it was perceived by many to be pagan and thus unsuitable for a Christian country. However, its formal grandeur and elegance appealed to some early railway tycoons, mainly because it represented power, stability and permanence. For this reason, classicism was popular with northern industrialists, and therefore with some railway builders in the north of England. Conventionally symmetrical and adhering to the rules and orders laid down by the architecture of Greece and Rome, classicism was used in the Victorian period with considerable freedom. Styles of the ancient world featured alongside the classicism of the Renaissance, and in many cases were adapted for different materials. The building that set the standard for the pure classical style was Philip Hardwick's great portico for Euston, wantonly destroyed in the early 1960s. This was echoed in Birmingham and in many other places but, at the same time, a more informal and relaxed classicism was developed for railway stations that simply drew in a general sense upon Italianate and Renaissance models. By this means, stations great and small all over Britain could be called classical in a general way, and this tradition was maintained well into the 20th century, with some fine 1920s and 1930s neo-Georgian examples.

▲ Completed in 1850 by the LNWR and Lancashire & Yorkshire Railway, Huddersfield is Britain's most magnificent classical station. A mass of columns, colonnades and pilasters, it has the look of a grand country house.

▼ With a style determined by the city it served, Bath Green Park, seen here in 1959, is a pure statement of classical symmetry. Built by the Midland Railway, completed in 1870 and closed in 1966, it was the link between the industrial north of England and the south coast.

▲ Nottingham's Central, or Victoria, station was only loosely classical, reflecting as it did a mix of French and Italian Renaissance elements. Completed in 1900, it was closed in 1967 and subsequently demolished, leaving only the clock tower to survive as a famous city landmark.

◄ G T Andrews, a close associate of George Hudson, the 'railway king', designed many stations for the York & North Midland Railway and developed a characteristic domestic style of Italianate classicism for small stations. A good example is Castle Howard, built in 1845 and now a private house.

► In the 1920s a simplified classical style became popular with image-conscious railway companies because it gave a sense of modernity and elegance. For the same reason, the style appealed to architects of post offices and government buildings. This is the new station at Clacton-on-Sea, completed in 1929 by the LNER, a company keen on the classical neo-Georgian style.

UNDER THE CLOCK

NTIL THE COMING of the railways, time in Britain was a movable feast. Bristol time and London time were at least ten minutes apart but it never mattered as travelling was such a slow process. With trains it all changed and time, and timetables, had to be standardized. Railway companies adopted Greenwich time and by 1852, thanks to parliamentary acts, this was established throughout Britain. Indeed, Greenwich time came to be known as railway time. As a result, stations had clocks, generally in prominent places or grand architectural settings. In effect these represented the first large-scale development of public clocks in Britain. With public clocks came new concepts of time-keeping, making punctuality both a duty and an important element in social life. The ability to meet beneath the station clock changed for ever the domestic pattern – and, more significantly, romance.

▼ The Manchester, Sheffield & Lincolnshire Railway made its way into Hull via the ferry across the Humber from New Holland. Its Hull terminus was, therefore, a station without a railway, known as Corporation Pier. Its rebuilding in 1880 was marked by a prominent clock.

▼ All that remains of Nottingham's Victoria station, opened by the Great Central Railway in 1900, is the great Renaissance-style clock tower, still looking magnificent despite its drab modern surroundings.

▲ Buxton had two stations side by side, operated by independent companies. This clock on its decorative iron bracket, still in place in 1968, underlined the need for good timekeeping.

▲ Opened in 1841 and enlarged in 1883, Brighton's terminus station is still splendid. The four-faced clock is proudly surmounted by the monogram of the London, Brighton & South Coast Railway.

◄ While not strictly a railway clock, the splendid iron clock tower outside Holyhead station reflects the Victorian fascination with the regulating and display of time.

▲ A handsome clock tower adds a decorative touch to the functional brickwork of Kings Cross station in London.

◄ So many meetings, assignations and romances must have started, and ended, beneath the clock at London Waterloo.

COTTAGE AND DOMESTIC

With no traditions to follow and well away from the big-city style wars, the builders of rural railway stations were free to follow their own ideas and develop their own styles. Many country stations had to combine railway functions with the domestic needs of the stationmaster or staff. Architects and builders were influenced primarily by vernacular details, materials and cost. The result is a nationwide legacy of individual and often idiosyncratic local station buildings that range from the basic to the extraordinary, a wealth of cottage-style structures that express the diversity, imagination and practicality of the railway age. Some simply looked like cottages or small domestic houses that happened to have a railway purpose, while others were created specifically and distinctly as railway buildings. Since the closures of the 1960s many of the former have become purely domestic, losing in the process any tangible railway associations but becoming satisfactory small houses. Materials were often local, and decorative details, where the costs allowed them, could echo regional traditions. However basic, the staffed station was an outpost of the railway company it served, and its appeal to passengers was of fundamental importance. Small stations were therefore generally well maintained, with comfortable rooms, plenty of seating and fires in winter inside, while outside gardens and flowers enhanced the cottage feel.

▲ Photographed in the late 1960s, Hope station still has the look of a small timber cottage although its style is typical of the basic staffed station all over Britain. The chimneys and the windows add to its domestic look.

▼ In April 1964 tank locomotive 1445 pulls its single carriage into Berkeley station, en route from Sharpness to Berkeley Road Junction, in Gloucestershire. A single passenger waits, emerging from the rather grand station, which is not unlike a lodge of a big country house.

▲ The Darlington & Barnard Castle Railway opened in 1857, serving a remote region, with stations that looked just like cottages. This is Gainford, in stone with barge-boarding; it has in fact been a cottage since its 1960s closure.

▲ More chalet than cottage, Charlbury, in Oxfordshire, is a relatively original Brunel wooden country station of 1853, characterized by the hipped roof and pronounced eaves. This famous example has retained most of its GWR features today.

20th CENTURY AND MODERN

In the early 20th century railway companies became increasingly image conscious and keen to dispel any hangovers from their Victorian past. This was the era of fast travel, named trains, Pullman comfort and modern marketing. Distinctive house styles and branding were part of this modernization process, all greatly accelerated by the formation of the Big Four in 1923. Of greater importance, however, was the major upgrading of stations and railway buildings. In the Edwardian period stations had begun to reflect the popularity of Arts & Crafts styles, particularly in the newly developing suburbs. In the 1920s a refined and simplified classicism became fashionable, but far more significant was the impact of modernism in the 1930s. All over the network concrete and geometry came together with dynamic effects as the Big Four competed in their determination to present a modern image. The GWR initiated an extensive rebuilding programme, to be seen at Cardiff, Paddington and elsewhere, but more extreme was the Southern and its architect J R Scott, who brought a distinctive Art Deco look to stations such as Bishopstone, Surbiton and those along the line to Chessington South – places that reflected the modern image of the Southern Electric network. This was brought to an end by World War II, and by the time station rebuilding started again in the late 1950s, a new kind of modernism was emerging, with plenty of glass and metal used with brick or concrete, as seen in stations like Banbury, Harlow, Stafford, Chichester and Coventry. Some have not worn well, some are still memorable. The 1960s were characterized by concrete brutalism, but since the post-modernist, high-tech era of the 1970s and 1980s there has been a return to more sensitive, expressive architecture.

▲ In 1947, just before nationalization of the railways, the GWR published *Next Station*, their vision of the future. This included visionary designs for a number of stations, in styles that blended Art Deco with 1950s modernism. This classic design for Weymouth, with its great clock tower, would have brought the Victorian station up to date. It was never built.

▼ This is Abbey Wood station, east of London, a building whose parabolic roof exemplifies the more adventurous architectural styles that, in the late 1970s and 1980s, began to emerge from the long shadow of naked concrete modernism. From this moment modern engineering and the use of contrasting materials combined to change the nature of station architecture.

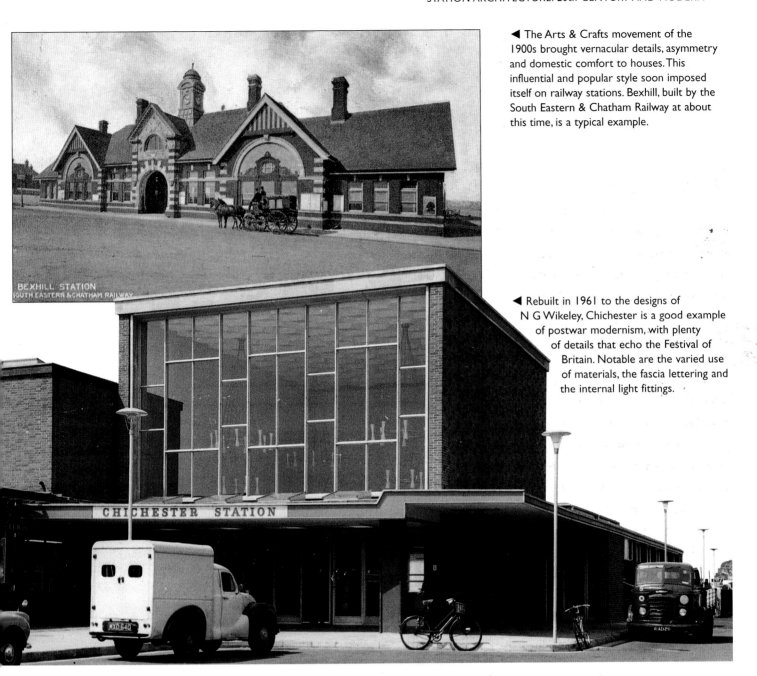

◀ The Arts & Crafts movement of the 1900s brought vernacular details, asymmetry and domestic comfort to houses. This influential and popular style soon imposed itself on railway stations. Bexhill, built by the South Eastern & Chatham Railway at about this time, is a typical example.

◀ Rebuilt in 1961 to the designs of N G Wikeley, Chichester is a good example of postwar modernism, with plenty of details that echo the Festival of Britain. Notable are the varied use of materials, the fascia lettering and the internal light fittings.

▶ In the late 1930s the architect J R Scott brought Art Deco, modernism and cinema-style geometry to the Southern Railway. This is Malden Manor, one of a group of four matching stations on the branch to Chessington South. Curving cast-concrete platform canopies match the dramatic style of the exterior. Rather surprisingly, these four stations survive, largely unchanged, as a memorial to the Southern's aspirations towards modernity.

IRONWORK

ARCHITECTURAL cast iron is one of the wonders of the Victorian era and it was the adventurous use of this material, for stations, bridges and other structures, that was the practical foundation of the railway age. Cast iron was first used as a building material in the 18th century, but it really came of age from the 1830s. Great strength and stability, combined with rich decorative detail, made it the perfect material for the vast trainshed roofs of the early stations, such as Paddington or York. However, it was equally suitable for many other uses, including canopy supports, signal and lighting posts, fences, gates, benches and notices. For bridges and other load-bearing and flexible structures it was soon replaced by wrought iron, but in all other areas cast iron remained king. Thus, decorative cast iron is one of the most distinctive products of the railway age. Its legacy is still to be enjoyed all over Britain.

▲ Built originally to mark a junction, Hellifield gradually became the centre of a substantial railway community. The present station, dating from 1880, is notable for its decorative cast ironwork.

▼ The great iron train sheds combined great structural strength with delicate cast detail and rich colours. This is Liverpool Street, in London, built in 1875 and sensitively restored in the 1990s.

▲ Cast-iron spandrels and canopy supports were ideal for the decorative display of railway company initials and monograms. Many survive to be enjoyed today. This is the Taff Vale Railway's monogram at Porth station.

▲ Cast- and wrought-iron fencing outside Marylebone station features the initials of the Great Central Railway, the station's builders, who completed this, London's last terminus, in 1899.

▶ A vast, once-busy station dating originally from 1847, Tynemouth is now served by the Tyne and Wear metro system. It was rebuilt in 1882 when the acres of cast iron-supported canopies were added.

BRICKS AND MORTAR

In the early days, stations were often insubstantial structures, frequently made from wood, but railway companies soon learned that they needed to give passengers, and shareholders, a sense of permanence and stability. Initially, design and construction was in the hands of engineers, some of whom - notably Brunel – managed to turn themselves into competent architects. However, faced with the need to design and construct large numbers of diverse buildings at speed, the railways quickly understood that they needed real architects as well. A number of companies forged long-lasting relationships with architects of note, for example George Andrews with the York & North Midland, Henry Hunt with the North Staffordshire, David Mocatta with the London & Brighton, and Sir William Tite with the London & South Western. Many architects made significant contributions to the success of the developing railway network, some working to a formula, others approaching each building individually. The result was a wonderful diversity of architectural style, matched by an equally diverse approach to materials. In the end, the determinant of what a station would look like and how it would be built was the budget, and this was driven by traffic projections which, like all projections, were often wildly inaccurate. Wood was extensively used, for speed, cheapness and convenience. However, for durability and that vital sense of permanence, brick and stone were preferred, usually sourced locally. The result is a rich legacy of inventive regional architecture, making the station a remarkable creation of the Victorian era.

▲ Built in a typically Victorian polychrome manner from red brick, with blue and white bricks for decoration, Ockley is a domestic-style station near Dorking, in Surrey. This type of straightforward brick station was to be found all over Britain, varied only by the details and the type of bricks used.

▼ For the LSWR's line west from Salisbury Sir William Tite designed a standard Tudor-inspired station. A number survive, the best being Axminster, a decorative blend of soft-coloured brick and stone detailing. Mullions and gables echo local architectural traditions. Recent restoration has returned the station to its 1860 look.

► Timber island stations, with extensive windows, curved roofs and shingles, are a feature of the West Highland Line. Some, such as Rannoch Moor, one of Britain's most remote stations, have matching signal boxes on the platform.

◄ Dowlais Cae Harris, a typical Victorian country station on the Valley lines in south Wales, was built from local stone ornamented with quoins and details in a contrasting white stone. Some buildings survive.

▲ Cark & Cartmel station was rebuilt in 1862 in a kind of Swiss chalet style, with timber-framing on a local grey limestone base and a decorative canopy. Regular use by the Duke of Devonshire inspired the extravagance. Sadly, although the station is still open, the building does not survive.

WISH YOU WERE HERE!
THE WEST COUNTRY

RAILWAY STATIONS *were popular subjects for postcards from 1904 onwards, and photographers seem to have been assiduous in capturing as many as possible before World War 1. Major termini, city and town stations, quiet country halts, all were grist for the photographer's mill, or rather lens. Many were taken at quiet moments and carefully posed accordingly. It is remarkable how often the photographer actually stood on the tracks. Others took an elevated position whenever it was available. Trains are rarely the focus of attention, though they do feature quite extensively in this selection from the south-west of England.*

▶ *Radstock, in Somerset, had two stations, North, on the Somerset & Dorset line, and - seen here - West, on the GWR line from Bristol to Frome. This picture shows the power of the photographer: the train waits and everyone stands still for the camera.*

◀ *This card of a GWR railmotor at Dawlish Warren Halt, in Devon, was posted in 1907. It was a minor station in a remote location to the east of Dawlish, built largely for holiday business. No station was too small or insignificant for the postcard photographer. Inevitably, these are the ones that appeal most to collectors today.*

◄ Considering the busy nature of Bristol Temple Meads station, this postcard photographer must have taken his life in his hands for this shot.

► Penzance was always a busy station, particularly in the holiday season. As can be seen on this card, it had only two platforms, which caused operating problems. Also visible is the 1870s train shed. The card was posted in 1908 by Janie to Darling Johnny: 'Just a card to let you know I love you. Hope you will answer by return. 14 kisses.'

◄ Originally Milborne Port Halt, Milborne Port was a surprisingly substantial station east of Sherborne on the Waterloo to Exeter line. Making the most of a quiet moment, the photographer has lined up all the station staff by the signal cabin, and has then set himself up in the middle of the tracks.

THE STATION COMPLEX

▲ Cast-iron footbridges were made in many forms and styles. This one was at Hockerill Halt, on the Great Eastern's Bishop's Stortford to Braintree line. Footbridges made good viewing points for trainspotters.

▶ A station like Highbridge in Somerset was a busy complex, with several signal boxes, sidings and goods yards, and an engine shed. The prefabricated concrete footbridge is typical of many railway components factory made in that material from about 1910.

▼ In the summer of 1959 a local train bound for Exeter pauses at Tiverton, dwarfed by the massive covered footbridge whose twin stone towers look like some medieval fortification.

Early stations were simply booking offices, sometimes with goods facilities, but this basic structure was soon greatly expanded to suit the needs of passengers and freight. Waiting rooms and lavatories arrived, and later refreshment rooms and shops, turning the station into a complex of related activities, either on the platforms or adjacent to them. However, even in the early days, the station rarely stood on its own. Near by, or incorporated within the building, was the stationmaster's house and other offices and facilities catering for various staff needs. Many stations also had signal boxes, to control the movement of trains through the station and in and out of its sidings. These were generally sited carefully to allow the signalman a clear view of the track but could either be independent structures away from other buildings or linked into them. Smaller signal boxes stood frequently on platforms or on iron supports raised above the platforms. They could also on occasion be placed on bridges. Many signal boxes were two-storey structures, with the lower storey housing the machinery or sometimes acting as a lamp store. Large stations could have two or more boxes.

Small stations often had only one platform, used by trains in both directions, but it was far more common for there to be two or more platforms. Initially passengers were expected to cross the tracks from one platform to another but this was soon deemed to be dangerous and platforms came to be linked by footbridges or tunnels. The footbridge is a characteristic piece of railway architecture and there are many variations: open or closed, timber, cast-iron, steel or concrete. Some

designs are unique to a particular railway company. Many stations had water towers or columns, for servicing steam locomotives and these could be found in a variety of forms and designs. Although the steam age ended decades ago, many water towers are still to be seen. Another common feature was the coal yard, usually adjacent to a siding close to the station, but this was for domestic and industrial users and not normally for locomotive use, except at terminus stations, where there might also be an engine shed.

▲ In 1962 the long-arm water column, serving both tracks, and its associated water tower were still in use at Llantwit Major on the Vale of Glamorgan line. Since then the station has been closed and reopened, but the column and tower have gone.

All but the smallest stations had a goods yard and usually a goods shed, a reflection of the fact that for a century from the 1850s the railways were the prime movers of goods and freight of every possible description. A goods shed enabled the transfer of merchandise from one wagon to another, the loading and unloading of wagons, and exchanges between road and rail to be carried out smoothly and under cover. A goods shed might have one or more access tracks, with doors at either end to enable wagons to be shunted in and out. Inside, raised loading platforms and cranes facilitated handling. Loading platforms could also exist outside the goods shed, and

▲ Adams 4-4-2 radial tank no. 30583 waits beside the minimal engine shed at Lyme Regis, in Dorset. Single locomotive sheds of this type were frequently to be found at the end of branch lines, where the terminus station and its related buildings were often fairly substantial.

◄ GWR tank locomotive no. 5500 shunts goods at Perranwell station, in Cornwall, in 1959, marshalling a line of box wagons that are to be loaded or unloaded in the adjacent goods shed, which has two access tracks. This type of activity was a daily sight at stations all over Britain until the late 1960s. The two ladies have just crossed the tracks, probably under the watchful eye of the signalman in his elevated box.

▶ A train from Spalding stands at Bourne station, in Lincolnshire, in the early 1960s. To the right is the large goods shed, with its warehouse on the upper floor. The scale of the building indicates that at one time this was the most important part of the station.

rural stations were often equipped with ramped platforms to simplify the loading and unloading of animals and livestock. Goods sheds might be simple structures in wood, iron and, later, concrete, or they might be substantially built from brick and stone, sometimes with decorative features echoing those of the station itself. A goods shed usually had a number of associated sidings for the marshalling of wagons. Larger sheds could be linked by crane or elevator to railway warehouses, built for the storage and handling of commodities such as grain, wool, cotton, beer, wines and spirits and tobacco. These were generally large buildings, constructed to be secure and fireproof. All over Britain goods sheds survive adjacent to stations, either disused or adapted to non-railway activities, a lasting reflection of the importance of goods traffic and how it made the station such a vital component in the local economy.

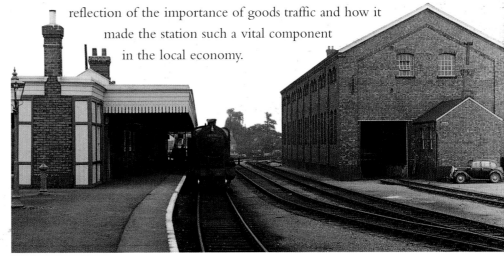

WHY DID WE GO THERE?

PENZANCE is Britain's most westerly station. It opened in 1852 but it was not until the completion of the main line from London a few years later that the town, as well as west Cornwall as a whole, began to attract visitors. A network of branch lines and ferry services to the Isles of Scilly quickly opened up the region and made accessible to thousands its unique blend of coastline, landscape and history, while at the same time encouraging local industries. From the 1870s artists were spreading the appeal of Cornwall to a wider world.

4237 **G.W.R.** **TO** **Penzance**

▲ Posted in 1909 by a visitor from Lancashire, this card shows Penzance's main street on a quiet day. The message refers to the 'lovely weather', one of the factors that explains the enduring appeal of west Cornwall.

▲ No visitor in Cornwall in early May would miss the Helston Furry Dance, shown here. Access was then easy via the Helston branch line.

▶ Perennially popular with visitors, the First and Last House had long been an essential stop on the tourist trail when this card was sent in the 1930s. There was no train to Land's End but plenty of buses reached this then remote spot.

THE FIRST AND LAST HOUSE – LANDS END

◄ The changing view of St Michael's Mount is one of the pleasures of the last few miles of the train journey to Penzance. As a result, it has always been a popular postcard subject. This view, with the causeway at low tide, was posted in 1908. 'Isn't it a lovely place,' says the writer, from Durham.

St. Michael's Mount.

THE
ISLES OF SCILLY

► Cornwall has always been a county of legends, many of which were marketed to visitors. Not least was the Polperro Pisky: this is the lucky Pisky Well, haunted by ghoulies and ghosties.

DIP YOUR "POLPERRO PISKY" IN THIS WATER FROM THE LUCKY ALL SAINTS' WELL'

'THE PISKY WELL' CORNISH GHOULIES AND GHOSTIES HAUNT POLPERRO, CORNWALL

FOR SUNSHINE AND NATURAL BEAUTY
TRAVEL BY RAIL TO PENZANCE, THENCE BY BOAT, R.M.V. "SCILLONIAN", TO ST. MARY'S
ACCOMMODATION ENQUIRIES TO THE CLERK OF THE COUNCIL (DEPT. 'P')   BRITISH RAILWAYS

▲ The special quality of the Isles of Scilly brought many visitors to Penzance in order to take the ferry. British Railways wanted them all to come by train, hence this 1950s poster.

► In the 1920s the fishing village of St Ives became an artists' colony, resulting in many colourful cards.

STATION STAFF

MEN AT WORK

The railway industry included a great number of different professions, many of which were highly skilled. Some were adapted from other areas of commercial activity but the majority emerged with the industry, for example drivers, firemen, signalmen, stationmasters, shunters and guards. Initially, many were recruited from the army and navy and from the mining industry, and this set the tone. Railway staff were generally strong, literate and loyal, independently minded but conscious of being part of a family, many professions united within an industry famous for stability and longevity of service, often over several generations. At their peak, the railways employed over 650,000 men and women, all of whom were more individual in their attitudes than workers in any comparable industry, yet linked by their sense of community. For this reason, people from the railways attracted the interest of photographers from the early days, a reflection of the fact that they were seen broadly as a breed apart. There are thousands of images of unknown railway men and women by largely unknown photographers, from the 1850s onwards, sometimes posed, sometimes taken informally, and these are the pictures that tell, better than anything, the story of a great industry.

▲ Many early railway employees came from the police, and there have always been railway police. This man is on duty at the 1975 Shildon steam cavalcade, which celebrated the Stockton & Darlington Railway's 150th anniversary.

◄ A member of the staff, perhaps the stationmaster, at St Bees, on the Cumbrian Coast line, pauses for the camera in the 1890s.

▲ A young railwayman, perhaps a porter or shunter, stands casually by the track at some unknown location in the 1930s. With hands in pockets and cap askew, he wears a classic long-sleeved jerkin with the statutory watch and chain.

◄ Immaculately turned out, confident and proud of his job, a shunter poses for the camera in the 1960s. He clutches the long pole used for hitching and unhitching the couplings and is directing the driver of the class 08 diesel shunting locomotive with clear hand signals.

► Issued originally by the Central Office of Information in 1951, this photograph shows Harry George of Monmouth, a railway employee who then worked full-time at Troy, one of Monmouth's two stations. His job included wheel-tapping and looking for faults on the wagons in the goods yard. In his spare time he worked as a town councillor, 'an ordinary man doing an ordinary job ... proud enough of his town to spend the whole of his spare time running it'.

WOMEN AT WORK

Despite widespread belief to the contrary, women have always worked in the railway industry. Before the 1860s there are records of rural station mistresses and women working as booking clerks, crossing-keepers and even as navvies. However, women were mostly employed in areas deemed suitable for them: in hotels and refreshment rooms, in offices as clerks, typists and telegraph or telephone operators, in workshops as seamstresses and polishers, and as cleaners. Anything regarded as men's work was closed to women. Nevertheless, some 13,000 women, about 2 per cent of the workforce, were employed by the railways before World War I but inevitably were paid less than men in equivalent positions. World War I changed everything, and by 1918 over 50,000 women had filled jobs vacated by men joining the forces and were working as porters, ticket collectors, crane operators, van drivers and in many other hitherto male positions. However, pay rates were still far from equal, despite union efforts in support of women employees, and when the men returned from the war, many women were simply dismissed. Those who remained, in the traditional female roles, faced inequalities in pay and service conditions and restrictions on employment after marriage. By 1939, 26,000 women worked for the railways, mostly in offices. World War II changed everything again and, by 1944, 114,000 women were working on the railways, 75,000 being in male positions such as guards and factory machinists. About 400 were killed by enemy action while on duty. After the war, most women were once again dismissed from male jobs, but from 1958 equal pay and opportunities legislation began to come into force. Today, women work in all areas.

▲ The only operational position open to women from the late Victorian era was crossing-keeper, and many filled this role in rural areas, as wives of railwaymen. This lady was in charge of a crossing on the old Cockermouth & Workington Railway.

▲ In this World War I image, a lady railway employee sits surrounded by male colleagues, who clearly show little resentment towards her. The station is Torphins, a remote place on the Ballater line in Scotland, so they may well have known her before she was employed.

◄ The sight of women railway workers in uniform became familiar in World War I, but they were not always accepted as equals by male colleagues. This photograph, taken at Stretton in Derbyshire, seems to have been posed to show women at work. However, the men, except for the one close to the lady who is not in uniform, are keeping their distance.

▲ The impact of World War I as a force for social change is reflected in this photograph of two railway employees posing as equals. They could be husband and wife, father and daughter or simply colleagues. In any case, they are content to be seen together on 6 March 1919.

◀ A lady crossing-keeper and pointswoman poses for the camera at Cadhay, near Ottery St Mary in Devon, in about 1910. The onlookers underline the fact that, at this date, this was an unusual sight.

STATIONMASTERS

In Victorian Britain a stationmaster enjoyed power, prestige and respect, not only among his employees but also in the wider community. He was the sort of person who could be asked for a reference. His responsibilities were considerable and included the daily operation and maintenance of the station and all the related paperwork, the proper use of equipment, stores and supplies, the management of staff and the correctness of their turnout and appearance, the maintenance of good relations with passengers and the encouragement of business and the promotion of the railway company, of which he, or very occasionally she, was the public face. In different railway companies stationmasters were sometimes known as agents, superintendents or, on small stations, clerks, while today the term station manager has become fairly universal. In the past, stationmasters were also housed by the railway company and were relatively well paid, factors that increased their status within the community. In the mid-Victorian period, a stationmaster's annual salary ranged from about £60 to about £250, the latter for a big city terminus, and there were bonuses, gratuities and other benefits, such as presents from local tradesmen. As a result, it was not unusual for stationmasters to stay in their posts for a long period, achieving in the process considerable local fame. Many of these figures were recorded by local photographers in images that celebrate the glory of the post and the uniform. During the 20th century the power and status of the stationmaster was gradually reduced, thanks to the spread of area and regional offices that took over the running of groups of stations, and today the post has virtually disappeared.

▲ By the 1960s stationmasters had become suited managers, but still enjoyed their status. This is Mr Clarke, stationmaster at Purley, in Surrey, photographed in 1965 in the modern signal box at his station.

▶ Victorian stationmasters were proud men who enjoyed their position and the uniform that went with it. Because of this, they were regularly photographed. Typical is this studio portrait of a Great Eastern stationmaster in about 1900, probably taken to celebrate his appointment to the post.

▼ 'A Happy Family – Patrington, E Yorks' is the title of this delightful Edwardian image of a stationmaster relaxing with his favourite dogs. Patrington was a small village station on the Withernsea branch, north of Hull.

▲ This Edwardian view of the staff of a station on the Taff Vale Railway underlines the power and status of the stationmaster. He sits in front of his staff, who stand in a row, almost at attention.

A HAPPY FAMILY - PATRINGTON. E. YORKS.

▲ The stationmaster of a London terminus was an impressive figure, still wearing top hat and tails when Eric Treacy took this carefully posed photograph at London's Euston station in 1955. Coronation class locomotive 'City of Coventry' is ready to depart but the driver has time for a final few words with the stationmaster while his footplate team look on.

RAILWAY INSTITUTIONS

FROM THE 1840s many railway companies were aware of the plight of railwaymen in need, and this awareness culminated in the formation of the Railway Benevolent Institution in 1858. Incapacitated railway workers, widows and orphans were among the beneficiaries. Some companies established their own orphanages, notably the Midland at Derby in 1875, later affiliated to the Railway Benevolent Institution. The best known was opened in Woking, Surrey, in 1885, later becoming the Southern Railway Servants' Orphanage. Another equally dedicated branch of railway benevolence was the convalescent home. The first of these, conceived by John Edwards Nichols, the chief cashier of the London, Chatham & Dover Railway, and partly funded by the philanthropist John Passmore Edwards, opened in Herne Bay, Kent, in June 1901. Others followed, at Leasowe Castle on the Wirral in 1911, at Ilkley Yorkshire, in 1915 and in Dawlish, Devon, in 1918. More were opened after World War I, including two dedicated to railway women, in Lavenham, Suffolk, and Margate, Kent. By 1947 the home at Herne Bay was handling 7,000 patients a year and by 1951, when it celebrated its golden jubilee, 41,500 had passed through its doors. Many railway institutions disappeared from the 1960s, their roles subsumed into the welfare state.

▲ Railway Convalescent Homes had their own standardized range of badged tablewares, specially made in Staffordshire. These examples date from the 1920s.

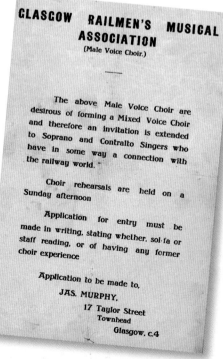

GLASGOW RAILMEN'S MUSICAL ASSOCIATION
(Male Voice Choir.)

The above Male Voice Choir are desirous of forming a Mixed Voice Choir and therefore an invitation is extended to Soprano and Contralto Singers who have in some way a connection with the railway world.

Choir rehearsals are held on a Sunday afternoon

Application for entry must be made in writing, stating whether, sol-fa or staff reading, or of having any former choir experience

Application to be made to,
JAS. MURPHY,
17 Taylor Street
Townhead
Glasgow. c.4

◀ Railway orphanages were dedicated to the education and entertainment of children in their care. Here in about 1910, a group of well-dressed orphans pose at Durham.

ALL FOR ONLY 2d. A WEEK

This message is especially addressed to those who are now entering the Service of British Railways, and are, therefore, not aware of the great work which is carried on by the Railway Convalescent Homes.

There are ten of these lovely Homes—six for men, four for women, and of these four for women one is reserved exclusively for women in Railway Service.

The Homes are maintained and managed entirely by the employees themselves. There is a Board of Trustees, assisted by various Committees, all of whom give their services voluntarily.

The benefits of the Homes are available to all in the Service who contribute regularly 2d. a week, and this can be paid through the paybills without any inconvenience to you. All you have to do is to sign the form at the back of this leaflet and hand it to your pay clerk. You can, of course, agree to pay more than 2d. a week if you so desire, and many do so.

Free travelling facilities to and from the Homes are granted to all railway employees and their wives.

Maybe you think you will never need help of this kind; but no one can guarantee good health, and, even if you could, you would be doing a great service to your less fortunate colleagues by becoming a contributor.

It should be remembered that the National Health Insurance Scheme does not provide this benefit, so you should protect your own interests by joining.

It should also be remembered that the above contribution covers not only you but, if you are married, your wife also, and if she has a baby under nine months she can take the baby with her.

The Homes are all situated in delightful surroundings; they are models of cleanliness; the beds are really comfortable, and the food is the best that can be provided.

If you are still in doubt get to know which of your Colleagues have been to the Homes and ask their advice. They will undoubtedly tell you to

BECOME A CONTRIBUTOR WITHOUT DELAY

Three months after the first contribution you are eligible for benefit.

IT IS NO USE BEING WISE AFTER THE EVENT

BE WISE NOW AND JOIN AT ONCE

CAS Ltd. 9R26M/JS3258/12.52

Herne Bay *opened 1901*

Dawlish 1918

Margate 1927

Llandudno 1950

FOUR HOMES ARE PICTURED ABOVE. THERE ARE SIX MORE JUST AS LOVELY

▲ Railway companies were always keen supporters of sports clubs, and there were many local and national competitions for activities as diverse as cricket, bowls, football and swimming. This is a ticket for the opening night of the boxing competition organized by the Sports Club at the Derby Locomotive Works.

▲ This 1952 Railway Convalescent Homes leaflet was produced to increase awareness of the homes and their services and facilities, and to encourage railway men and women to contribute a small weekly sum to a fund that, like an insurance policy, could be called upon in cases of need.

◄ Apart from supporting benevolent and welfare institutions, railway companies often encouraged their employees to join educational and recreational societies, such as the musical association promoted here.

41227. HERNE BAY: RAILWAY MENS CONVALESCENT HOME, SMOKING & SITTING ROOM.

▲ The most famous railway convalescent home was the one in Herne Bay, in Kent, and its popularity was reflected by the production of a number of postcards showing its buildings, interiors and gardens. This 1920s view illustrates the smoking and sitting room, with tables set up for dominoes and draughts.

Southern Miniature Railway
The Southern Railway Servants' Orphanage, Woking.

◄ A well-known and popular feature of the Southern Railway Servants' Orphanage in Woking was its miniature railway, shown here in a 1920s postcard. The smartly turned out driver shows off a gleaming scale model of a Lord Nelson class locomotive.

DRIVERS AND FIREMEN

Since the dawn of the railways, drivers have enjoyed a particular status, so much so that the names of the men who drove pioneering locomotives such as the 'Rocket' are well known. It is not surprising they were regarded as a special breed, highly skilled, working long hours in difficult conditions and carrying great responsibility, for both the train and its passengers. In the early days, drivers and firemen stood in the open and even by 1900 protection was limited and far from weatherproof. There were no seats until the 1930s, and the cab was a dangerous place, full of heat and sharp metal and bouncing about all over the place, while two men with separate areas of responsibility tried to work with some degree of harmony. To the end of the steam age little changed, yet there were always plenty of people wanting to be drivers. Training patterns were established in the early days: it was a long learning process, from engine cleaner to fireman and finally to driver. The switch to diesel and electric traction was part of a revolution that brought in single manning, automation, comfort, safety, efficiency and high-speed running.

▲ Well aware of their status, particularly towards the end of the steam age, drivers and firemen usually posed willingly when asked, as they frequently were, to be photographed. Typical is this crew, standing beside the old Southern M7 locomotive at Yeovil Town station in the late 1950s or early 1960s.

◄ This British Railways Western Region promotional photograph of the mid-1960s highlights the revolution in comfort, efficiency and safety represented by the switch from steam to diesel and electric power.

▼ After a few minutes on the platform at Ryde Pier Head station on the Isle of Wight, the driver returns to the cab at the front of the former London tube train, one of a fleet of similar vehicles that work their retirement on the Island Line's route to Shanklin.

► Many crews operated on a shift basis, with regular changes along the route. Here, at Swansea High Street in the 1960s, the up Pembroke Coast Express, headed by Castle Class 5054 'Earl of Ducie', is handed over to a new crew. The locomotive could take on water, or be changed, as the train passed through various regional boundaries. In the early days drivers tended to stick to one engine but by now it was all 'common-user'.

▲ In 1949, in the early days of British Railways, a final discussion takes place somewhere in the Southern Region between driver and stationmaster. The young fireman looks on, knowing that departure is imminent. This photograph, issued by the Railway Executive Committee, was designed to show the importance of people – about 635,000 men and women – in the brave new world of nationalized railways.

SIGNALMEN

A fter the train driver, the most familiar figure in popular railway lore is the signalman, solitary in his box over long hours of day and night and in all weathers, controlling the safe passage of trains. Initially policemen controlled signals, while dedicated pointsmen looked after the points. With the introduction of interlocking and block systems, it all came together under one man, working in a specially built cabin or box and responsible for one length of track. The application of complex rules and regulations, and meticulous recording of all train movements and all messages sent or received, were the signalman's responsibility. He made decisions on prioritizing trains, particularly at junctions and on busy lines with a mix of freight and passenger services. And the weight of the levers meant the work was also physically demanding. Larger boxes had more than one member of staff but most signalmen had to be capable of working alone on long, often antisocial shifts. Yet it was a vital job, and offered considerable status to those who could manage the lifestyle. In the 1930s there were over 26,000 signalmen; with modern technology the number of signal boxes, and thus signalmen, has been vastly reduced.

▲ Signalmen tended to be a particular breed of man, self-contained, at ease with his own company and able to enjoy the particular qualities of the job. Often they were friendly towards visitors, like this jolly chap at Scout Green, near Shap, photographed in the 1970s.

▶ A glorious study of the signalman at Longhope station box, in Gloucestershire, as he makes himself a cup of tea on 20 November 1963. The nature of the job meant that signal boxes had to be warm, comfortable and equipped with basic catering facilities.

▲ Until the 1970s, signal boxes, and signalmen's duties, had changed little since the Victorian era. In most boxes, points and signals were still controlled by heavy levers, and messages were sent and received via telegraph block instruments. This classic view shows the signalman hard at work in his box at Desford Junction, in Leicestershire, on 4 May 1963.

▲ Mr Richards, signalman at Binegar on the Somerset & Dorset railway, posed in his box for Ivo Peters, one of Britain's best-known railway photographers, in 1953.

WISH YOU WERE HERE!

SOUTHERN ENGLAND

RAILWAYS IN SOUTHERN ENGLAND were always wonderfully varied, with stations serving city termini, commercial centres, resorts, the commuter belt, military camps and remote rural towns and villages. Postcards document this diversity, with very few stations in this accessible region escaping the photographer's lens. As a result, station postcards are living history, a moment in time frozen for ever and becoming in the process fascinating social history a century later. The photographers, invariably anonymous, took great care with the construction of their images and, as ever, the trains are incidental.

▶ Brighton station opened in 1841 and was rebuilt in the 1880s, though retaining much of its original quality. A seaside terminus demanded an excellent iron train shed, and that is what Brighton got. The Edwardian photographer chose a moment when the platforms were full of carriages but not much was going on, perhaps around midday on a Sunday.

Brighton Station

◀ A local railmotor sits in the platform on a sunny day in Bournemouth Central in 1913. Opened in 1885, the station is marked by its magnificent train shed, worthy of a terminus rather than a through station, and one of the best in Britain. Fully restored in 2000, it looks, remarkably, much the same today.

◄ There were plenty of military lines and military stations in southern England, especially in the Salisbury area. This 1914 card shows Bulford, which was not in fact a military station but was on the branch line that served Bulford Camp, via Amesbury. The message, from a soldier in the Hampshire Regiment at Bulford Camp to his sister, says: 'I heard that Arthur had a little scrap with the Germans. Don't I wish I could get to the front and have a pop at them.'

► A train approaches Camberley, Surrey, in 1910. The morning rush hour has passed and the up platform is packed with ladies on their way to London, perhaps meeting their friends for lunch or going shopping. A porter stands by a trolley loaded with parcels, ready to put them into the guard's van as fast as possible.

Camberley Stati

TENTERDEN CHURCH & STATION

◄ A rural railway par excellence was the Kent & East Sussex line from Robertsbridge to Headcorn. It opened in 1905, so Tenterden station was still quite new when this card was sent in 1913. The place is deserted - but then it was never a busy line. Today, the station lives again on a preserved steam railway.

KEEP THEM RUNNING

While major train-servicing operations are carried out in the depot, there is always plenty to be done on a day-to-day basis at stations. In the course of their daily work, steam locomotives needed to take on water regularly, and this was normally the fireman's duty, using the platform water tower. Other maintenance and servicing operations for locomotives were carried out at the start and finish of each journey, but coaling was done 'on shed'. The advent of the diesels made life much simpler for train crew and station staff, though occasional maintenance was still required. More demanding was the constant and never-ending task of keeping carriages clean and tidy. The carriage exterior and windows had to be washed, for decades by hand. The interiors had to be tidied and accumulated rubbish, most of which had been left by passengers, had to be removed. The internal water tanks had to be filled and the lavatories and basins cleaned. Lavatories did not become general on trains until the 1890s, though some royal carriages were equipped with chamber pots and washing facilities by 1848. Until the 1980s lavatories flushed directly on to the track, using water held in roof tanks. Now all train lavatories have to flush into retention tanks below the carriages, which in turn have to be emptied at the station at the start or end of the journey. Catering requires constant servicing as restaurant and buffet cars are restocked and rubbish is removed. This process has been simplified by the widespread use of the mobile trolley system, but even these require restocking after every journey. Finally, destination and route notices have to be replaced and reserved seat tickets allocated.

▼ Even diesels can need water. Here, in May 1962, type 4 no. D108 tops up its train-heating boiler at York, using the water supply designed for steam locomotives.

◄ Automated carriage-washing facilities existed only at depots and some major stations, so at most stations there was still much to be done by hand. On 13 October 1965, with closure imminent, the carriage window cleaner is still hard at work at Highbridge, in Somerset.

► While passengers come and go, the tank locomotive of a Western Region railmotor is watered at Saltash, in Cornwall, in 1959. At that time this was still a very common sight at stations all over Britain.

◄ Little railways need servicing too. Here, probably in the 1950s, station staff at Aberystwyth have a jolly good sort-out of the guard's compartment on a Vale of Rheidol narrow gauge carriage.

▼ 'Finished With Water' is the caption on this photograph. A schoolboy in a striped blazer looks on while, cigarette in mouth, the fireman of rebuilt West Country class locomotive no. 34044 'Woolacombe' pulls the hose from the platform water tower away from the tender.

SMILE PLEASE!

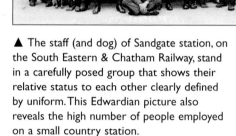

▲ The staff (and dog) of Sandgate station, on the South Eastern & Chatham Railway, stand in a carefully posed group that shows their relative status to each other clearly defined by uniform. This Edwardian picture also reveals the high number of people employed on a small country station.

Railway workers have always been a distinctive and individual breed, members of a close-knit community with its own strong rules and traditions. From the early days it was regarded as a respectable profession, and the railway companies were generally seen as good employers, even if the rates of pay were low. Uniforms were supplied, and many railway workers lived in company houses, particularly in remote locations. Railway communities often had their own churches and schools, education being an important principle in the railway industry throughout the Victorian period. Other benefits included privilege tickets and cheap coal. As the network expanded, the numbers of employees rose dramatically, from 47,000 in 1847 to over 365,000 in 1884. When British Railways was formed, the total was 690,000, a figure that has steadily, and significantly, declined ever since. Even a small station would have several employees and a major terminus could have hundreds. The railway was widely regarded as a kind of family, and in many cases generations of the same family followed each other into the industry. At the same time, it was a very hierarchical industry, with clearly defined positions, regulations and routes to advancement. These hierarchies were often defined by uniform, the infinite varieties of which had echoes of the military. More than in a other industries, railway workers seem to have enjoyed posing for photographs by both amateurs and professionals, a reflection of their sense of pride and kinship.

▼ Verwood, in Dorset, was a typical small town station when this photograph was taken in about 1910. Station staff stand on the platform, complete with dog, while the platelayers stand on the track, their area of responsibility.

▲ Byfield was a station near Woodford Halse, in rural Northamptonshire. The photographer has taken great care with his placing of the staff, trying to identify them by position and activity. Perhaps they are, from left to right, signalman, stationmaster, clerk, two porters.

▶ In a typical Edwardian photograph a young stationmaster in a smart overcoat poses on an unidentified GWR station, flanked by two of his station staff.

▲ Somewhere on the LNWR four ill-assorted railwaymen have been persuaded to pose for the camera. Three of them, including the stationmaster look a bit reluctant. However, they have gone to the trouble of moving the very heavy station bench across the platform. As ever, in these photographs, there are neither trains nor passengers.

▶ In this late Victorian photograph of a group of staff on the platform of Instow, a LSWR station near Bideford in Devon, relative status has been carefully defined by position, with the stationmaster well to the front. Instow station was closed in the 1960s, but parts have since been restored, and a section of track relaid.

PASSENGERS

TAKING THE TRAIN

assengers were first conveyed by train in Britain in 1807, along the Oystermouth Railway, which ran for 5 miles beside Swansea Bay in south Wales. This pioneering line, known later as the Swansea & Mumbles Railway, had opened in 1806 for goods traffic, which was carried in horse-drawn wagons. Its proprietors had no interest in passenger carrying and contracted this out to an independent operator. This attitude was common among early railway companies. The Stockton & Darlington, for example, contracted out its passenger business from 1825 to 1833; the Liverpool & Manchester did run passenger services, but its main interest lay in freight traffic. The general view was that passenger carrying was a waste of time and money.

This was soon to change as it became apparent to many operators that income from passenger traffic could be equal to, or even exceed, that coming from freight. In the 1840s various Acts of Parliament controlling the price of tickets gave a huge boost to passenger carrying, along with the gradual disappearance of the horse-

▲ As captured by the casual photographer, passengers, the lifeblood of the railway, show their true diversity. These gentlemen were photographed at precisely 12.05pm on 28 September 1920, location sadly unspecified.

▲ The passage of BR Standard class 5 no. 73029 through Knowle & Dorridge station, near Solihull, in August 1959 should not distract the eye from the two splendidly hatted commuters waiting on the opposite platform. It is a lovely day but they have their umbrellas just in case, and they would feel undressed without them.

► There is a period quality to this photograph of passengers waiting to have tickets checked at the barrier at London Waterloo. It is the summer of 1970, as evidenced by the clothes. The train is for Portsmouth Harbour and no doubt some of them are on their way to the Isle of Wight, with holidays beckoning.

◄ The photograph is captioned 'Platform 9 at Bristol TM in March 1961'. King class locomotive no. 6027 'King Richard I' simmers in the background, but it is all about the lady striding along the platform in her high heels, making light of her bags. Why has she been at the end of the platform, normally the province of trainspotters and mailbag handlers?

drawn coach services on roads that hitherto had been the only way for most people to travel around the country. Thus, from the late 1840s, the railways began to concentrate on passenger traffic, developing in the process a nationwide network of trains that had precedence over the slower freight services. From the 1860s the roles were reversed in many parts of Britain as freight revenues soared and exceeded passenger income year by year until 1914. However, by that time the pattern of large-scale passenger carrying was well established and the railways had made their way into every corner of the country and into every aspect of daily life. By the end of the 19th century passenger services had improved immeasurably. Carriages were larger, more comfortable, safer and equipped with facilities such as lavatories. Dining cars had appeared, and express trains were also travelling much faster. By now there were two distinct types of passenger traffic, long-distance and suburban or commuter, and the railway companies had to adjust accordingly. The short-distance commuter business caused particular problems, with all the travel bunched into short periods at set times of day, and established operating patterns that have dominated urban railways ever since.

The vision of universal travel that the railways offered the Victorians was in every sense revolutionary. Its impact is described in the novels of Charles Dickens and can be seen in paintings such as W P Frith's *Paddington Station*. The railway revolution affected everyone, impinging on family and social life, on trade and

▼ Period cars and a period British Rail scene as passengers leave the 14.08 Reading to Bedwyn DMU service in July 1976. The flares and the hairstyles say it all.

▲ All of Edwardian railway life is here in this 1906 postcard of the Brighton train leaving London Bridge: girls with dogs and bicycles, family farewells and lovers' partings, the newsboy and the porter with the mailbags. Naughty Gertie writes: 'This puffing billy is bound for the seaside!'

▲ 'Student photographers record the demolition of Bedford St John's station in April 1971 in preparation for closure' – so reads the photographer's caption. Railway enthusiasts of all ages travelled widely in the 1960s and early 1970s to capture such images.

▶ On an early summer afternoon in 1974 the guard from the single car DMU from Bristol to Severn Beach belatedly checks the tickets of passengers who got off at Montpelier.

business and on leisure activities. More importantly, it brought together people of widely differing social backgrounds who would never normally have met, let alone travelled in a train together. It was to meet this challenge that a distinct class system began to emerge. At the start, the terms first class and second class were applied to trains rather than passengers, and referred to their speed. However, they were quickly transferred to the passengers, to ensure satisfactory social segregation. This went as far as separate ticket offices and waiting rooms, as well as carriages. Soon, third class appeared, applied initially to those travelling in open wagons. There was even a fourth class for a while, to identify those travelling in especially cheap trains, while the pattern of travelling to work encouraged the running of special workmen's trains, at early hours, for the benefit of the 'labouring classes'. At the other end of the scale, extra charges

▶ In a scene reminiscent of a Frith painting, crowds wait on platform 9 at Bristol Temple Meads in the 1930s. So many stories to tell: the sailors, the schoolboys, the uneasy lovers, the smart young men, the ladies on shopping trips, the tough businessmen, the railway staff who have seen it all before, so many times…

▼ Bath Spa station in the 1950s, a decade defined by the Vauxhall and the Rover and by the flouncy skirts, petticoats and hairstyles worn by the two girls. Where are they going? Shopping in Bristol, off dancing, meeting friends, waiting for a date? Who knows?

▲ This Edwardian scene at Somerton station, in Somerset, is unusual because the photographer has not tried to pose the picture. As a result, it is informal amd immediate, with most of the passengers paying no attention to the camera. Only the guard looks straight into the lens. With the drifting steam, it is an emotive image, like a still from a film.

were applied for certain express trains, creating a kind of super first class. The management of all this was immensely complex, but it was a mirror of Victorian society. However, the railways did break down social barriers and by the 1880s the system was going into reverse. Companies started to abandon second class, and to even out the distinctions between first and third. By 1914 over 90 per cent of passengers in Britain were travelling third class. This pattern continued through the 20th century and still applies today, although the distinctions have been blurred by nomenclature and the adoption of confusing definitions such as first, business, standard and so on. In modern, egalitarian Britain passengers have become customers, and no one is allowed to be called second class, despite the complexity of contemporary ticket prices, and the minefield that it represents to the unwary or the inexperienced.

Since the 1980s passengers and their needs have dominated the railways, and the number travelling on British trains seems to increase year by year. In the beginning, the railways forced dramatic changes upon a society largely unaltered since the early 18th century by bringing large-scale travel into existence. Once acquired, this habit has proved impossible to give up, and subsequent generations have used the railways in ever greater numbers and show no sign of doing otherwise. Passengers may complain continuously but, like it or not, they still need the railway and the railway needs them, in their wonderful diversity.

▲ Three elderly but elegant people pose for the camera in the 1920s, the lady in her fur coat looking flirtatiously over her shoulder, her companions looking disdainful. The caption is simply Conway Valley, so perhaps it is Llandudno Junction and the two men have come to say farewell to the lady.

▲ This 1988 image of the concourse at Glasgow Central is full of activity and interest. There are as many stories to be told as there are classic platform views. The temporary greenhouses bring a new dimension to station retailing, while the pod information kiosk is a period piece.

▼ A busy summer scene at Haven Street on the Isle of Wight in the early 1960s as two local tank engines meet, W27 'Merstone' coming in with a Cowes train and W14 'Fishbourne' waiting to depart for Ryde Pier Head. A member of the station staff holds up the single line token, watched by a young lady and her baby. Are they passengers or have they come to watch father, or maybe grandfather, at work?

WHY DID WE GO THERE?

BRIGHTON, with its reputation as a resort well established by the 1820s, was an obvious early railway destination. The London & Brighton completed its line in 1841 and the town and its surroundings immediately took on a new lease of life. Ever-expanding holiday, excursion and commuter traffic resulted in the station being much enlarged in 1883, by which time Brighton was busy with traffic from at least four directions. It may have had a slightly raffish reputation, but for the discerning traveller it also had the Brighton Belle and the route to Paris from Newhaven.

167 (34a)

London Brighton & South Coast Railway.

TO Brighton

▲ Brighton was one of the first railway excursion seaside destinations and, as this 1963 handbill indicates, the habit continued for decades.

BRIGHTON SERIES.   BOOTS. NOTTINGHAM.

On the Sands

Brighton.

▲ Brighton's universal appeal was based on its premier position as a seaside resort. Its own beach was stony, but there were plenty of others all around and easily accessible by train and bus. This card of about 1903 shows children on the sands, bare-legged but otherwise well dressed.

▶ The best way to travel to Brighton from London was on Britain's most famous commuter train, the all Pullman Brighton Belle, which ran between London Victoria and the resort from 1933 to 1972.

10430. "Brighton Belle".   British Railways Photo.

Stanmer, Nr. Brighton.

◀ Away from the hurly-burly of Brighton, a different world awaited the visitor. All around the town was rural Sussex at its best, lovely countryside with plenty of sleepy villages, all easily reached by train, bus or bicycle. This 1920s card is from the 'Sleepy Sussex' series.

THE CLIFFS ROEDEAN BRIGHTON

▶ Saucy postcards galore underlined Brighton's raffish reputation. This example was the strange choice of a small boy to send to his aunt!

"BY GUM, JANE, WHAT BRINGS YOU HERE?"
"I'M LOOKIN' FOR A HUSBAND!"
"BUT YOU'VE GOT ONE!"
"WELL, THAT'S THE ONE I'M LOOKIN' FOR!"

AT BRIGHTON

▲ To the east of Brighton the coast rises into spectacular cliffs, culminating in the Seven Sisters and Beachy Head.

▶ Dieppe was the destination for ferries from Newhaven. For decades this was the most fashionable and the most direct London to Paris route.

151 DIEPPE. — Le Train de Paris et la Malle. — LL.

DESTINATIONS

STATIONS ARE the beginning and end of journeys, and journeys are taken for many reasons: duty and necessity, pleasure and relaxation, love and adventure, even fantasy. Stations offer choices and the bigger the station, the greater the range of choices. Everyone must, at some point, have stood below a big departure board at a major city terminus and been tempted just to take a train and go. All stations are destinations, but the magic and romance lie in the big journeys to distant parts of the network, offering exciting views of places and landscapes hitherto unseen. Ideally, such journeys involved named trains, hauled by locomotives bearing special headboards hinting at the nature of the journey and its destination. Today, such trains are rare, with only a few famous names, such as the Flying Scotsman, lingering in the timetable. However, the railways of Britain still offer great journeys and great destinations. Penzance to Aberdeen is the best.

▲ The old departure board at Waterloo came through World War II but by 1976 it was due for replacement. The new board, in the same location, served for nearly 30 years before it too was replaced by modern electronic screens. The journeys remain much the same.

►▼ Route books were issued by several companies in the 1930s. *The Track of the Royal Scot*, with this striking cover was in the LMS series. The Royal Scot was still running 20 years later (right). In 1950, two pioneering diesel electrics, 10000 and 10001, rest at Euston.

"WHO RUNS MAY READ"

The Track of the Royal Scot
(Part I)

LONDON (EUSTON)
TO
CARLISLE

Illustrated description
of the Journey

PRICE ONE SHILLING

LMS Route Book No. 3

◀ Amid steam and smoke the Flying Scotsman, headed by a Deltic diesel, is ready to depart from London Kings Cross in the 1960s. The headboard is being slotted on to the front of the locomotive.

THE HULL PULLMAN

HULL
Retford
Doncaster
Goole
Brough

C

▼ Many stations were equipped with fingerboards that indicated platform and destination. A famous example was at Bath Green Park, seen here in August 1962 with its equally famous operator, Joyce Ainsworth. Train times were chalked at the top of the board. Joyce is holding the board for the Pines Express, one of the best-known trains on the Somerset & Dorset line, about to depart for Bournemouth West, its final stop.

▲ The Cambrian Coast Express was a famous 10.10am weekday service from Paddington for Aberystwyth and Pwllheli. In June 1963 it paused at Shrewsbury, with 7821 'Ditcheat Manor' in charge.

HALF-FARE

Children and trains are inseparable. Generations have been brought up on train books, notably the Thomas the Tank Engine series, and toy trains. Children are fascinated by trains, they watch them, they like the noise and the atmosphere, and even modern children seem to understand the appeal of steam. In the past, trains were central to children's lives. Children went to school by train, on holiday by train, to the shops, cinemas and coffee bars by train. Many became train fanatics, standing in groups or on their own on busy platforms, efficiently writing down the number of every train that passed. They went on journeys with friends to hidden corners of the network, to track down elderly branch lines and ancient locomotives long past retirement. They travelled on children's tickets, half-price to the age of 14, and then it was all over. They left school and started work or went to college; now it was the real world and the trains became a means of getting from A to B. As adults, they also did their courting by train, but that is another story…

▼ Immersed in their own world, three schoolgirls chatter their way along the platform at Dymock station, on the Gloucester to Ledbury line, in July 1959, without a thought for the unusual 1930s GWR railcar that has brought them there.

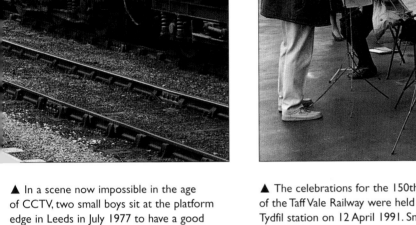

▲ In a scene now impossible in the age of CCTV, two small boys sit at the platform edge in Leeds in July 1977 to have a good look at the big Deltic locomotive across the tracks.

▲ The celebrations for the 150th anniversary of the Taff Vale Railway were held at Merthyr Tydfil station on 12 April 1991. Smart locomotives attended and a local school orchestra played on the platform.

▶ Three classic young rail enthusiasts pose for a friend's camera on the platform at Burghclere station, in Berkshire, in the 1950s. They can take their time, for the station is deserted and the line from Newbury to Winchester Chesil was never very busy.

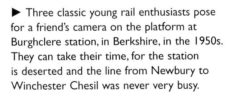

▲ It is early September in 1961 and there is plenty of activity on the platforms at Taunton, in Somerset. Some Girl Guides, unsmiling, are on their way home from summer camp, two small boys run about in front of the photographer, and on the locomotive the fireman leans out of the cab window, looking the other way and waiting for something to happen.

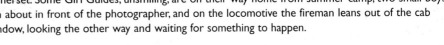

TEN MINUTES AT PADDINGTON

ON THE MORNING of 3 June 1927 a photographer working for the Great Western Railway's publicity department took up his position, looking down on platform 1 at London's Paddington station. His job was to record everything that happened in the minutes leading up to the departure of a scheduled express. From the many trains leaving Paddington every day, the GWR managers had selected one of their most famous, the Cornish Riviera Express, whose 10.30am departure was a fixed point in the timetable for decades. The anonymous photographer took a sequence of stills over at least a ten-minute period, with the focus on the constantly changing nature of the crowds on the platform, while the train remained a fixed diagonal across the image. Platform 1 has always been the most important at Paddington, with its clock and access to the shops, offices and facilities that flank it, so many of those captured in the photographs would have been using the platform as a thoroughfare, or idling and waiting but not necessarily catching the train. The three images shown here span ten minutes, with the first at 10.20, the second at 10.28 and the third at 10.30. Some people appear in all three, while others have come and gone, giving the sequence a cinematic quality. It is a remarkable record of life at a major London terminus.

Below: 10.20 – most doors are open and leisurely conversations take place beside the train. Passengers for this and other trains walk up and down, businessmen, elderly travellers and families. A group of schoolgirls pass by. Everyone is well dressed. Top right: 10.28 – doors are closing but parcels and luggage are still being loaded. The unhurried conversations continue. The crowd has thinned and families fill the foreground, on their way to other parts of the station. Lower right: 10.30 – the whistle has blown, the doors are shut, the train begins to move and final farewells are made. Those not taking this train wander on past. Meanwhile another train has drawn into platform 2.

A DAY OUT

▲ By the 1970s excursions were sometimes just a means of encouraging weekend travel, in this case from Oxenholme in May 1974.

Railway companies began running special trains from the 1830s. These were most notably for those attending race meetings but other, earlier users of these services were temperance and religious societies and mechanics' institutes. By the 1840s these specials had become both widespread and regular, and so the excursion train was born. In 1844, for example, the London & Brighton Railway began to operate regular excursions along its route, seeing this as a profitable way to increase business. Other companies followed, and the traffic increased steadily, particularly at Easter and in the summer. Excursions could be day trips over short distances or longer journeys taking many hours, with participants sleeping on the train. The emergence of the travel agent greatly expanded excursion traffic, despite the fact that the carriages used were often primitive, uncomfortable and overcrowded.

Excursions were run for all sorts of reasons. In 1849 an excursion train from London carried its passengers to Norwich to watch a public execution. The Bank Holiday Act of 1871 brought a further increase in excursion traffic, by

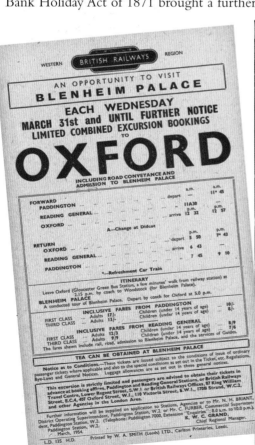

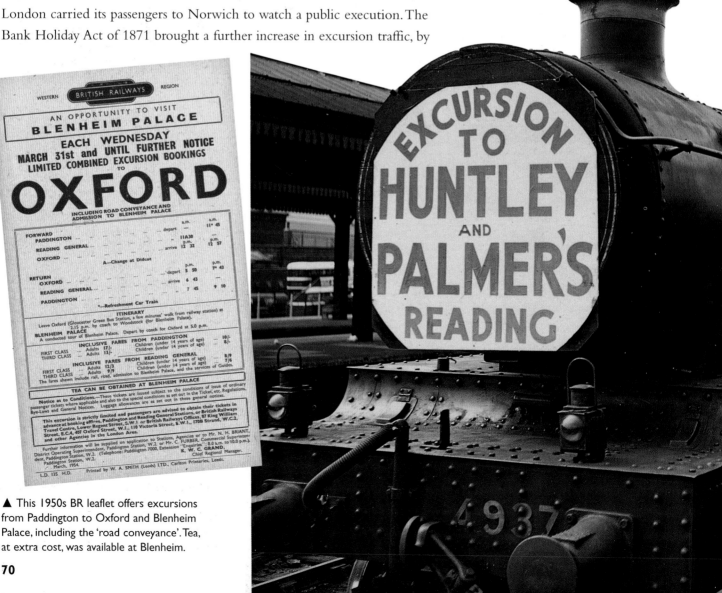

▲ This 1950s BR leaflet offers excursions from Paddington to Oxford and Blenheim Palace, including the 'road conveyance'. Tea, at extra cost, was available at Blenheim.

▲ Edwardian holidaymakers, using a scheduled service for a seaside excursion, descend from a GWR railcar for a day by the sea at Dawlish Warren, in Devon. Typically well dressed, they probably used the special day outing excursion fares that were offered by many railway companies.

GRAND EASTER HOLIDAY
LOCOSPOTTERS' EXCURSIONS
from LONDON
ON THURSDAY APRIL 26th 1962 TO
DONCASTER WORKS
Fare: 22/6 Under 16;   45/- Adult
KING'S CROSS   Depart: 10.10 a.m.   Return: 7.11 p.m.

from LONDON
ON FRIDAY APRIL 27th 1962 TO
SOUTHAMPTON DOCKS
Visits to BALCONY OCEAN TERMINAL
DOCK LOCOMOTIVE DEPOT · DOCK MODEL ROOM
and
SWINDON WORKS
Fare: 21/- Under 16;   42/- Adult
WATERLOO   Depart: 8.10 a.m.

The trains will include a buffet car from which light refreshments can be obtained. A limited amount of accommodation will be reserved for adults, or adults accompanying not more than one child. Please specify if you wish to use this accommodation. Juveniles need not be accompanied by an adult. The train will be supervised by our own staff and guides will be provided on the tours of the Works. It is regretted that bookings for visitors to join the party at the Works cannot be accepted as the trips are limited to those travelling on the special trains.

.... USE THIS BOOKING FORM ....
TO   DONCASTER*   EXCURSION
SOUTHAMPTON SWINDON
Craven House, Hampton Court, Surrey.

Please send..
*LONDON to DONCASTER ....ADULT tickets from
LONDON to SOUTHAMPTON & SWINDON   for which I enclose remittance of
: s. d.
NAME ....
ADDRESS ....

Tickets will be available in April. Please enclose 3d. stamped addressed envelope.
Bookings will not be acknowledged unless a stamped addressed postcard is sent.
* Delete whichever is inapplicable.

▲ Excursions to railway workshops have long been popular. Southampton docks and Swindon works on the same trip must have seemed good value to the trainspotters on this 1962 outing.

◄ Happy children and ladies in flowery frocks seem to be enjoying their outing to the biscuit factory, as they pose by no. 4937 'Lanelay Hall', the GWR locomotive that has brought them to Reading on a sunny day in the 1930s.

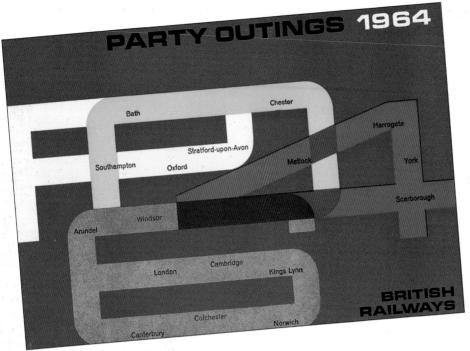

PARTY OUTINGS 1964

Chester
Bath
Harrogate
Stratford-upon-Avon
Southampton   Oxford   Matlock   York
Scarborough
Windsor
Arundel
Cambridge
London   Kings Lynn
Colchester   Norwich
Canterbury

BRITISH RAILWAYS

◄ Dynamic design underlines British Railways' promotion of party outings in this 1964 brochure. Inside are many suggestions for an organized party using scheduled services – a Thames cruise, Constable country, Coventry cathedral, Lorna Doone country, the Wye valley, Blackpool's seaside, Scottish islands, even no-passport trips to the Continent. The party organizer travels free, provided there are 25 taking part, and party catering offers packed meals in carrier bags or a small meal tray.

which time standards of safety and comfort had been greatly improved. At the same time, companies began to take their employees on outings to the seaside. A famous example was the Great Western Railway's annual Swindon Trip; in July 1914, 26,000 people left the town for the day. Excursions and outings remained a major railway business through the 1920s and 1930s, with sporting events and seaside trips heading the popularity table. After nationalization, excursions began to diminish, although they retained their popularity on a more local level and continued to be promoted through the 1970s and early 1980s, many combining rail travel with road or sea outings, or with entrance to exhibitions, museums or country houses. At the same time, party travel was increasingly promoted, to encourage small groups to use regular services instead of special or excursion trains. Today, dedicated excursion trains are rare.

► The train has pulled into the platform at Blackpool Central and a crowd of day trippers amble towards the exit. In late Victorian and Edwardian England, Blackpool was an immensely popular resort, catering for holidaymakers from the industrial towns of Lancashire. In the season, long holiday excursion trains awaited their turn at the crowded platforms, each one pouring its hundreds of remarkably well-dressed visitors into the town and its pubs and on to its beaches and amusements. Each night the whole process was reversed.

Furness Railway.   WASTWATER.   SEASCALE STATION.

◄ Many railway companies encouraged people to use their excursion trains by publishing postcards of scenic destinations on their routes, in this case Wastwater, accessible from the Furness Railway's Seascale station.

▼ Outings organized by companies for their employees in all areas of business were common from the 1860s. Railway employees also made the most of outings and excursions. Here, a group of LNER commercial managers enjoy a day at sea in the summer of 1929.

BRITISH RAILWAYS BOARD (B)

SPECIAL PARTY

REGULATION TICKET

ONE PASSENGER

OUTWARDANDRETURN

8434

8434

Date of travel.....................

C.M.OUTING
15.6.29.

▲ Excursions were often organized and promoted by magazines and newspapers. Here, those taking part in an excursion organized by the *Stroud News* in about 1910 assemble at Stroud station, in Gloucestershire.

NIGHT-TIME

A BUSY STATION never sleeps. In the past, numerous services ran overnight, notably trains carrying mail, parcels, newspapers and milk. Some of these were included in the timetable as passenger services. Indeed, many are the literary heroes and heroines who have made the seemingly interminable journey home on the milk train. Today night-time activities are considerably reduced, but there is nevertheless something very exciting about the station at night, as trains depart for distant destinations. Sleeper services, which currently still run from London stations to Scotland and the West Country, are classic overnight services, maintaining even now the aura of romance and intrigue established by many famous films and books. On a more prosaic level, night-time is also an essential period for maintenance, servicing and repair, and major stations can be a turmoil of activity once the timetabled services have ended.

▶ The first proper sleeping cars ran between Glasgow and London in 1873. The network expanded steadily and in 1986, when this brochure appeared, it was still quite extensive, with six major routes linking places all over Britain.

INTERCITY SLEEPERS
THE JOURNEY OF A NIGHTIME

Valid from 29 September 1986

InterCity

▲ It is 20.05 at London St Pancras on 13 November 1990 and soon the 20.10 mail will leave for Derby, headed by a class 31 diesel locomotive. The station is alive and scheduled services wait to depart but at this moment there is no one to be seen.

▶ Night-time at Leeds in February 1990 and the setting is strangely quiet and empty. The unloading of the luggage van of the HST 125 diesel is nearly finished but work has temporarily come to a stop.

◀ The Gothic towers, battlements and pinnacles of Bristol Temple Meads are best seen at night, when floodlighting accentuates the glorious theatricality of the façade. It looks as exciting in 1980, when this photograph was taken, as when the building was completed in 1878.

ROMANCE

I n countless books and films and through decades of real life, the station has been the setting for meetings and partings, and for romantic assignations of every kind. Joy and sorrow, love and passion, hope and despair, argument and reconciliation are all part of life's daily pageant on every large station as couples act out their own private dramas amid the hurly-burly of the crowded platform. Lovers meet and separate, in the manner captured for ever by the film *Brief Encounter*, their lives driven by the timetable and the station clock. Stations witness tempestuous emotions, placid love, devotion and desperation in equal measure, and so many awkward, final exchanges take place over cups of coffee or at the barrier while the train, indifferent and impersonal, waits to depart. Generations of newly married couples have set off on their honeymoon by train, and then returned some days or weeks later to face the reality of marriage. So many affairs and holiday romances have spluttered into indifference and vain promises at that moment of parting on the station platform. Yet, for all that, the station remains uniquely a place in which romance can flourish.

"SAFE—FOR AN HOUR AT LEAST!"

This Picture illustrates a dramatic incident in the great New Story starting in "ANSWERS," for week ending October 31st, Of all Newsagents and Booksellers.

▲ This Edwardian postcard advertises a forthcoming drama in the magazine *Answers*. Amid the swirling snow, as the train races through the wild countryside, the dashing heroine drags the handsome escaped convict into the warm privacy of her compartment. What happens next…?

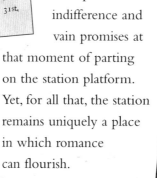

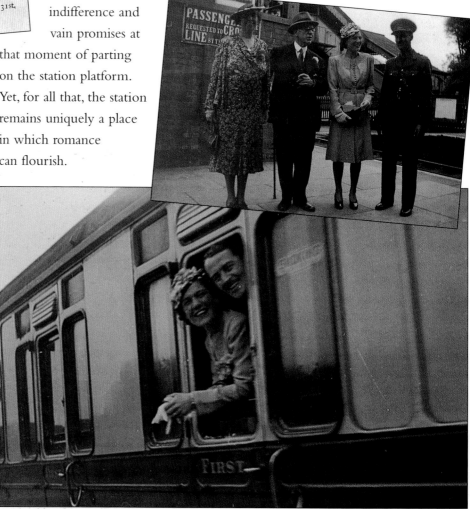

▶ It is a wartime marriage and a small group has gathered on the platform of some GWR station. The happy couple and, probably, her parents stand in line for the photograph taken by the best man or perhaps the stationmaster. The couple then lean from the window of their first class compartment as the train departs, she clutching her gloves and looking radiant, he looking cheerful and relaxed.

▲ Trains still play a part in many weddings and plenty of couples opt for the romance of the steam train at preserved railways all over Britain. This happy bride posed for her photograph at Totnes station in 1993, on the Dart Valley Railway, in Devon.

► In October 2002, making the most of the independently run buffet at Axminster station in Devon, this couple decided to have their wedding breakfast on the platform before starting their honeymoon on the train to London Waterloo, en route for Morocco. The weather smiled on them.

ALONG ROYAL LINES

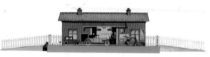

Queen Victoria was the first monarch to travel by rail, in 1842, and from that date she was a regular train traveller. She used royal trains for domestic journeys, to Scotland and the Isle of Wight, and elsewhere for formal occasions, but more important was her extensive use of train travel as a means of showing herself to her people in relative comfort and security. As a result, she became the first British monarch to be familiar to all her subjects. For her journeys she used the various royal carriages and trains built for her by different companies. There were also a number of royal stations, at Windsor, at Gosport for the Isle of Wight, at Whippingham for Osborne, at St Margarets in Edinburgh, and at Wolferton for Sandringham. These were rarely exclusively for royal use but all had private royal areas and facilities. Likewise, there was a suite of royal waiting rooms at Paddington and other main stations used regularly by Queen Victoria. Subsequent monarchs, Edward VII, George V and George VI, continued to use the royal trains extensively for both private and formal journeys, but the royal stations were gradually given up. Through the 20th century stations continued to witness many royal and State occasions, for example the reception of foreign dignitaries arriving by train from Channel ports, the arrival of royal parties carrying out various formal duties, the great State funerals, as well as the journeys by the royal family on private business. The present queen was a regular train traveller early in her reign but now the royal train, although it offers excellent security and privacy, is rarely used.

▲ King George V and Queen Mary arrive at Rochdale station in 1913 on a tour of the north-west of England. They visited various industries, including the Doulton potteries at Stoke-on-Trent and the railway works at Crewe. Stations receiving the royal train and the royal party were extensively decorated, the foliage at Rochdale being typical.

◄ The existing station at Wolferton, in Norfolk, was completely rebuilt in 1876 to cater for royal visitors to nearby Sandringham. There was a suite of royal waiting rooms and a porte cochère all in a vaguely Gothic style. In 1898 the line was doubled and a new set of Arts & Crafts timber-framed buildings, with more royal waiting rooms, was built on the opposite platform. This photograph shows these later buildings, soon after completion. The line to Hunstanton, which included Wolferton, closed in 1969 but the station buildings survive.

▶ On a royal visit in the early 1960s, Queen Elizabeth is greeted on the platform while other members of the party descend from the royal train. Pullman cars have been added to provide additional accommodation. Other dignitaries present include Prime Minister Sir Harold Macmillan, Alec Douglas-Home, then Foreign Secretary, and Princess Margaret.

▲ On 28 January 1936 soldiers carry the coffin of King George V towards the royal funeral saloon on platform 8 at London's Paddington station, while crowds watch in silence. The special train, hauled by GWR locomotive no. 4082 'Windsor Castle', then made the short journey to Windsor for the funeral and burial. In the past, stations traditionally played an important role in State funerals.

CENTRAL ENGLAND is a mixture of quiet, local stops vital to the rural economy and major stations and junctions serving passenger and freight trains from all over Britain. These contrasting elements of the railway network are caught in the images reproduced on postcards. Some photographers were commissioned by railway companies, some by postcard publishers great and small. Others worked for themselves, perhaps turning a hobby into a way of earning a living. What they all had in common was the desire to make the most of their skills, and their ponderous equipment, to get the best results.

WHITNEY STATION

▶ It is a wet day at Whitney-on-Wye station in 1912, a quiet place on the single line track near Hay-on-Wye. The photographer has picked his moment as the train approaches and, despite the weather, he has persuaded the few passengers to stand still in the rain so he can achieve the composition he wants.

Crewe Station

◀ When this card was produced in about 1910, Crewe was a huge station, one of the busiest in Britain. A rake of LNWR carriages stands in the platform, awaiting passengers and parcels but, apart from the cyclist and the distant groups of people, it is all rather static. It is a carefully structured image with a strong sense of perspective, yet it fails to capture the essential quality of this famous station.

Village of Rudyard, North Stafford Railway.

◀ Rudyard Lake was a scenic spot popular with day trippers from Stoke-on-Trent, who travelled there on their local North Staffordshire Railway. It was a busy line, on the NSR route to Manchester via Leek, through attractive Cheshire countryside. This Edwardian photographer has decided to show the village more than the station, but he has still taken the time to pose the station staff outside the signal box.

▶ The stationmaster watches as a train departs from Matlock Bath, Derbyshire, its steam and smoke merging with the mist that hangs over the heights ahead. The area was called Little Switzerland, so the Midland Railway chose a Swiss chalet style for the 1870s station. Prior to World War I, thousands of visitors arrived here for spa treatments.

Castle Station, Northampton

◀ Northampton had three stations. Bridge Street was the main LNWR one, and St John Street the Midland terminus. This card shows Castle Street, the third station, well to the north of the town on the LNWR main line. It was a plain building with an elaborate canopy. The photograph shows plenty of vehicles to take passengers into the centre of town.

TOWN AND COUNTRY

LONDON TERMINI

Railways arrived piecemeal in the capital, responding to a widely felt but unspoken belief, particularly in government and landowning circles, that the new monster should be kept out of the centre of London. As a result the marauding hordes, in the the form of the new railway companies assaulting the city, built their terminus stations in a circle around the centre. The major attacks came initially from the north and the west, in the form of the London & Birmingham and the Great Western, although a couple of smaller companies, the London & Blackwell and the London & Greenwich, had also mounted early assaults from the east. A ring of 15 termini developed, ranging in date from the late 1830s to the late 1890s. They varied considerably in architectural style, as well as in size, reflecting the ambitions and wealth of a number of railway companies. Each was distinct and separate, underlining the competitive nature of the railway business, and attempts at terminus-sharing generally ended in acrimony and disarray. For

similar reasons, most remained as termini, without connecting lines or lines that actually crossed London. Even today, lines across the capital are being discussed rather than built.

▲ When completed in 1866 to the designs of John Hawkshaw, Cannon Street was a magnificent station. Its hallmark towers and great iron roof survived extensive wartime bomb damage, as seen here in 1958, with West Country class 'Whimple' about to depart. Today, only the towers remain.

▶ This 1907 postcard shows the Hungerford bridge end of Charing Cross station. Opened in 1864, it reflected the ambitions of the South Eastern & Chatham Railway, which had been determined to have a terminus on the north bank of the Thames regardless of cost. Today, a 1991 building echoing its original shape rises over it, with the platforms squashed below.

◀ Nicholas Grimshaw's international station at Waterloo was completed in 1993, its wonderful curve a great addition to the more rigid formality of the original building.

▲ In the early 1960s British Railways issued *Facts & Figures* brochures about London termini, notable for their aerial photographs. This shows the 1906 roof of Charing Cross.

CHARING CROSS STATION

FACTS & FIGURES British Railways SOUTHERN REGION

G. E. R.

St. Pancras

The first major terminus was Euston but others quickly followed, albeit not always in their final location. For example, the end of the line for the Great Eastern was for some time at Shoreditch, the Great Northern ended briefly at Maiden Lane while Kings Cross was being built, and Nine Elms was a precursor to Waterloo. The major building periods were the 1850s and 1860s, decades that saw the emergence in their original form of Fenchurch Street, Paddington, St Pancras, Kings Cross, Victoria, Waterloo, Charing Cross, Cannon Street, Broad Street and London Bridge. Later came Blackfriars, Liverpool Street and Holborn Viaduct. Last of all were Marylebone, arriving in 1899 and barely fulfilling the ambitions of its builder, the Great Central Railway, and Baker Street, turned into a terminus in the Edwardian era by the equally ambitious Metropolitan Railway.

The 20th century brought little that was new but much rebuilding. In the 1920s Victoria's two adjacent stations, run by rival companies, were united behind their splendid Edwardian façades. Waterloo, by tradition London's most chaotic station, was totally recreated with exciting, elegant architecture and the most efficient layout in London. Others, such as Paddington, were enlarged and modernized. Wartime bombing damaged many London stations, but only Cannon Street was never to recover fully.

▲ Small boys, notebooks to hand, greet the arrival at Euston in the late 1950s of a Liverpool express, headed by Princess Royal class 46207, 'Princess Arthur of Connaught'. Today, health and safety concerns have sent such scenes into history.

▶ Although perennially busy with thousands of trains on weekdays, London's termini were always keen to promote weekend traffic. This December 1954 leaflet advertised excursions to places as diverse as Derby, Dudley Port, Rugby, Tamworth, Kettering and Leicester.

◀ Peak Class diesel no. 45110 hauls a long Sheffield-bound train out of St Pancras in 1976, beside the famous gasometers. The new international station has totally changed this view of Barlow's great train shed, which for years was the widest span in the world.

PROGRAMME OF

EXCURSIONS

FROM

EUSTON & ST. PANCRAS

FOR

SUNDAYS 5th 12th & 19th DEC. 1954

From EUSTON

	Third Class Fares s. d.		Third Class Fares s. d.
BIRMINGHAM, 5th, 19th	15/-	NUNEATON, 12th	13/6
BLETCHLEY, 5th, 12th, 19th	6/9	RUGBY, 5th, 19th	11/-
COVENTRY, 5th, 12th, 19th	12/9	TAMWORTH, 12th	15/-
DUDLEY PORT, 5th, 19th	16/6	WOLVERHAMPTON, 5th, 19th	16/6
NORTHAMPTON, 5th, 12th, 19th	10/-	WOLVERTON, 5th, 12th, 19th	7/9

★ BOOKINGS ALSO FROM WATFORD JUNCTION ★

From ST. PANCRAS

	Third Class Fares s. d.		Third Class Fares s. d.
BEDFORD, 5th, 12th, 19th	6/9	LOUGHBOROUGH, 5th	14/-
CHESTERFIELD, 19th	18/6	MARKET HARBOROUGH, 5th, 12th	11/-
DERBY, 12th	16/-	NOTTINGHAM, 5th	15/3
KETTERING, 5th, 12th, 19th	9/6	SHEFFIELD, 19th	20/-
LEICESTER, 5th, 12th, 19th	12/6		

★ BOOKINGS ALSO FROM ST. ALBANS CITY ★

CHILDREN under three years age, free; three years and under fourteen, half-fares.

The tickets are valid only on the date for which issued and by the services specified.
TRAIN SERVICES—from EUSTON Page Two; from ST. PANCRAS, Page Three.
FOR CONDITIONS OF ISSUE see Page Three.
Tickets can be obtained in Advance at Stations, Offices and Accredited Rail Ticket
Agencies; also certain Suburban Stations—see Page Four.

★ FOR FULL DETAILS ASK FOR PROGRAMME C218/R (H.D.) ★

Travel in Rail Comfort

BRITISH RAILWAYS

PLEASE RETAIN THIS PROGRAMME FOR REFERENCE

▲ A young trainspotter notes the imminent departure of A4 60015 'Quicksilver' from Kings Cross in the late 1950s. Behind him an old tank locomotive is ready to take recently arrived Pullmans to the carriage sidings.

G. E. R.

From_____

TO

LIVERPOOL ST. EXPRESS

◀ Broad Street was London's least-known terminus, yet its scale reflected the great ambitions of its creator, the North London Railway. By 1984, shortly before its demolition, it was little used by trains or passengers.

Then, in the 1960s, came the wanton destruction of Euston station. One of the greatest architectural achievements of the railway age was replaced with a structure of total mediocrity, infamous worldwide for its lack of style and utter disregard of passenger comfort. Luckily the outcry saved the other great Victorian termini, and changes in the 1980s were more sympathetic. Broad Street, the least-used of all London termini, disappeared but in the process its neighbour Liverpool Street, another famously chaotic station, was magnificently restored. Holborn Viaduct and Blackfriars ceased to operate as termini, but Fenchurch Street and Charing Cross were changed in dramatic fashion when new buildings were erected on top of them, in New York style. This also happened at Cannon Street, but without the same architectural verve. In the 1990s the great hotel frontage to St Pancras, under threat of destruction for years, was finally saved and restored, and in 1993 London acquired its first major new terminus, the international Eurostar station at Waterloo, a remarkable building in its own right, brilliantly attached to but independent of the existing station.

(37)
North British Railway.

King's Cross
(LONDON)

In 2007 the international emphasis will switch to St Pancras, with the completion of the restructuring of that great station and its hotel, and the addition of a new international station as exciting architecturally as the building to which it is attached.

Restoration projects have made many of London's termini look and work better than they have since the 1930s, but behind the modern developments, the cafés and the shops there is still that sense of achievement, history and quality that made them, in every sense, the cathedrals of their time. There is much to discover beneath the hurly-burly of daily use.

▲ On 22 August 1951 two immaculate and recently built Castle class locomotives, 7024 'Powis Castle' and 7025 'Sudeley Castle', rest at Paddington, having just hauled the royal train into the station. The ubiquitous small boys are present but, even then, scooter riding on the platform was not encouraged!

▶ Electric traction came to Paddington for the first time in the late 1990s with the opening of the dedicated Heathrow Express service, operated by smart class 332 units.

EUSTON STATION

IT IS NOW WIDELY acknowledged that the destruction in 1961 of the Doric portico and the Great Hall at London's Euston station was a supreme act of corporate vandalism, and largely unnecessary. Euston was the capital's first great station, and really the first great railway station in the world. Philip Hardwick's huge stone arch was a triumphal announcement to the world in 1838 that the railway age had arrived. The Great Hall was completed in 1849, adding architectural splendour to a setting that was already a grand spectacle. However, behind the pomp there was an unremarkable and mean station that became more and more confusing and dingy as it grew piecemeal. The LMS planned a total rebuild but was stopped by World War II. It was left to British Railways, who should have known better, to clear the site, despite a massive public outcry and questions in Parliament, and to build instead a bland station that works reasonably well but looks like an airport terminal. Ironically, the destruction of Euston was so unpopular that it probably saved London's other great stations.

▲ Seen here in 1960, just before its destruction, Euston's Great Hall was a splendid example of Victorian classicism, an incomparable expression of railway age ambition. The statue of Stephenson was saved and resited.

◄ This 1957 photograph shows the full scale and power of Hardwick's Doric arch and its flanking pavilions. Even to those who never saw it, the pointlessness of its destruction is obvious.

▲ This is the scene that greeted visitors to Euston once they had passed through the arch, an open square flanked on three sides by classical architecture. It was a generous space, able to handle taxis, cars and other vehicles with ease, despite its Victorian planning. Some of these photographs, and many more, were taken by British Railways in the late 1950s, as a record of the station they were about to destroy.

▲ In the 1930s the LMS struggled with Euston and tried to bring it up to date and make it more efficient. One of their additions was this smart Art Deco enquiry bureau, a dynamic structure woefully out of place in the middle of the Great Hall. It was removed in December 1952 and the Great Hall was returned to its Victorian splendour, with new enquiry offices placed discreetly on the building's right side. This sympathetic response to Victorian architecture was rendered meaningless when it was all destroyed nine years later.

◄ This 1948 photograph shows mail being delivered in the station's main square for the Irish Mail, at that point still the most important service operating out of Euston.

WHY DID WE GO THERE?

HARWICH had long had a harbour but from the 1860s it was greatly expanded by the Great Eastern Railway as a Continental port, serving Belgium, Holland and Germany. Traffic was such that it soon outgrew the old harbour and a new dock complex, named Parkeston Quay, complete with hotel, was built from scratch farther up the estuary. Harwich itself remained popular with visitors. It was a busy naval port and Dovercourt and Felixstowe offered resorts, beaches and hotels. Colchester and Ipswich, a short journey away via Manningtree, offered shops, museums and much else. Away from the coast, Constable country beckoned.

G. E. R.
Harwich

SPRINGTIME IN HOLLAND 1964

Enjoy a full day's **coach tour in bulb-land,** crossing by the British Railways Harwich-Hook of Holland night service

▲ The Harwich to Hook of Holland service was always the mainstay of the port. From the 1950s British Railways promoted it extensively, offering all-in holidays and short breaks, particularly during the bulb season.

Continental Steamer leaving Harwich

▲ This Edwardian card shows a night ferry leaving Harwich for the Continent on one of the busy routes that was developed from the 1860s. Although the card shows the Harwich skyline in the distance, ferries had been using the new facilities at Parkeston Quay since the mid-1880s.

► Ferries ran from Harwich across the estuary to Felixstowe, a popular resort in the early 20th century, thanks to its beaches and hotels.

◄ The bracing sea air of the East Coast was good for invalids, so there were plenty of convalescent homes in this region, notably in Felixstowe and around Clacton. Outings were encouraged as an aid to recovery. This resident wrote in 1935: 'Not able to walk very far so go by train.' The card shows that at this point there was clear sexual segregation.

► The architecture of the Essex and Suffolk borders offered much to the visitor. There were castles, churches and pretty villages to explore. Ipswich itself was a thriving town, combining new and old. A famous landmark was the Ancient House, shown here, whose walls displayed to perfection the local tradition of plaster decoration known as pargeting.

The Ancient House, Ipswich.

◄ Constable country lay inland, and Dedham was its heart, a few miles up the Stour valley from its estuary near Manningtree. However, this card, posted in October 1917, was not from an art lover, but from Bert, a soldier stationed at the huge Colchester barracks, to say he would be home on leave the next day.

CITY STATIONS

The opening of the Liverpool & Manchester Railway in September 1830 was an important milestone in so many ways, not least because it was built to connect two major cities. At one end of the line was Manchester's Liverpool Road station, the first in the world, still relatively complete behind its impressive façade and preserved as a museum. At the other end was Crown Street, Liverpool's original passenger terminus, reached by rope haulage from Edge Hill, where locomotives were attached and detached. Crown Street has gone but the present Edge Hill station dates from 1836 and is therefore the oldest station in Britain still in use. Other intercity lines quickly followed in the 1830s and 1840s, for example the London & Birmingham, the Newcastle & Carlisle, the London & Southampton, the Great Western to Bristol, the Bristol & Exeter and the Edinburgh & Glasgow, all of which featured important city stations. Indeed, railway companies were always ready to spend heavily on their city stations. The need to have

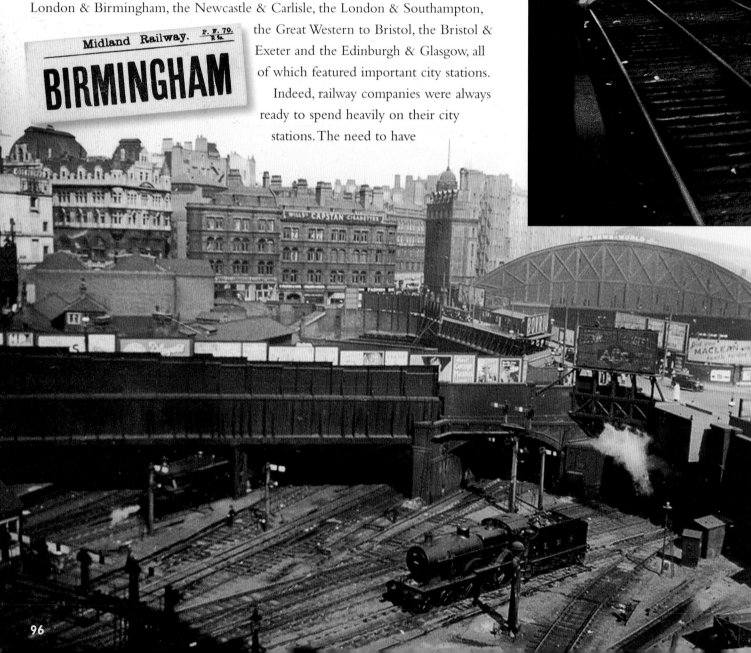

▲ The typical iron and glass train shed, seen here spanning the platforms at Birmingham Snow Hill in 1961, is one of the classic features of the city station. On a sunny day Western Region locomotive no. 7330 brings its long train to a gentle halt.

► One of England's best stations is York. Like Newcastle, it is built on a sharp curve, which in turn is echoed by the complex curving patterns of the iron and glass roof and the delicate flat-arched screens. York's first station was a terminus but this through station was completed in 1877. Nearly a century later, in 1971, it still looks dramatic and exciting as a train for Kings Cross prepares to leave, hauled by a class 47 diesel locomotive.

◄ The chaotic nature of Birmingham New Street is apparent in this 1920s view. Opened in 1854, New Street struggled for decades with expansion in a difficult site until it was, eventually, completely rebuilt by BR in 1967.

sites near the city centres, and the constructional difficulties inevitably associated with such sites, meant costs were bound to be high. At the same time, a city station was for a new railway company a major statement of intent, designed to generate a sense of permanence and stability, bolstering public confidence and thereby encouraging traffic. Architecture was very important, with the result that some of this first generation of city stations stand today as monuments to endeavour and achievement, for example Curzon Street in Birmingham or Temple Meads in Bristol. As the railway network expanded, more large towns and cities acquired significant railway stations whose adventurous architecture made the most of prime sites. By the same process, some cities acquired a number of stations, a reflection of the proliferation of railway companies. Indeed, there were in the end few towns or cities of stature in Great Britain that had only one station.

While there was no consistent architectural style, what many early city stations had in common was the enclosed train shed with a glazed roof spanning the platforms. Early examples in wood and wrought iron included Euston in 1837,

▲ As passengers idly await the London train, the sun shining through Stoke-on-Trent's ridge-and-furrow roof makes wonderful patterns on H A Hunt's Tudor-style curtain wall. The wall dates from 1848, along with the rest of this fine station and its matching hotel, but the roof is an 1893 rebuild.

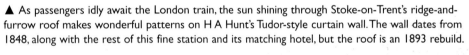

◀ Nottingham's station today is the former Midland station, a grand 1904 baroque and art nouveau extravagance. In May 1979 the St Pancras train, hauled by no. 45137, underlines the contrast between function and decoration.

▲ Influenced by Carlisle castle and law courts, Sir William Tite chose a Tudor style for the Citadel station, completed in 1850. This grey stone building carries the royal arms and the crests of the railways that commissioned it.

which set a pattern that was widely followed. The classic arched train shed came with the use of cast iron, with which the span could be steadily increased. In 1854 the single span at Birmingham New Street reached 212ft, and others soon matched this. However, the crowning achievement in this field was William Barlow's great span at St Pancras, 243ft wide and 110ft high. The glazed train shed remained a characteristic of major stations through the 19th century and one of the last was completed at Hull in 1904. Nearly a century had to pass then before another classic glazed train shed was constructed, at Waterloo International, by Nicholas Grimshaw, one of the few architects able to match the inventiveness and daring of his Victorian predecessors.

Rapid expansion of city stations through the Victorian period often resulted in piecemeal development, which in turn led to operating difficulties and passenger confusion. Engineers struggled to find solutions by using different platform layouts and by trying to combine termini with through stations. Brunel, always idiosyncratic, favoured a long single platform serving trains in both directions, made workable by complicated crossovers. Most were soon swept away but a similar system survives at Cambridge. In many situations the answer lay in total redevelopment, but few companies had either the money or the inclination to grasp that particular nettle until things became completely impossible. The rebuilding of

▶ This May 1977 view of the Edinburgh train leaving Newcastle shows the operating complexity of the modern city station built on early Victorian foundations and the difficult legacy of piecemeal development.

▲ Norwich City station, at the end of the meandering M&GN network, was, in city terms, a notably minimal terminus. In this 1914 view not a soul is to be seen, just baskets.

▶ When it opened in 1840, Brunel's train shed at his Temple Meads terminus set a pattern for city stations. In 1964, a year before it closed, mailbags await attention and a child is shown the pleasures of steam.

London Waterloo and Birmingham New Street are examples of drastic action forced by the threat of total chaos. In its architecture, engineering and operating diversity, the city station is one of the greatest legacies of the Victorian age. Most cities in Britain still have magnificent station buildings, even if some are now no longer in railway use. It is important to remember that until the 1830s there were no such things as railway stations and there was no architectural precedent. Early experiments in London, Liverpool, Manchester, Birmingham and elsewhere were, seen with hindsight, remarkably successful in establishing a building type that could be developed all over Britain, and indeed the world.

◄ City stations have to cope with many types of passenger, all with different demands. Inevitably, suburban services are often shoved into distant platforms or, in this case at Glasgow Queen Street, into the basement.

▼ Edinburgh's Waverley station fills a ravine at the heart of the city in a setting of architectural splendour, a glorious reminder of the power of the Victorian railway. Here, in 1971, with a Glasgow train departing, little has changed.

COMIC POSTCARDS

THE COMIC POSTCARD and the seaside holiday are inseparable parts of the British cultural experience. They grew up together, sharing a love of vulgarity and innuendo that goes right to the heart of the British character. The themes are predictable and universal and, remarkably, in these days of political correctness they all survive – as a glance at the postcard racks in any seaside resort will show. Favourite topics include marriage and domestic incompatibility, drunkenness and excess, obesity and sexism. Among the most popular settings are the beach, the hotel, the office or place of work, and the railway, the latter because of the direct link between railways and holidays. There are hundreds of comic railway cards, most of which follow certain themes: slow trains and delays on the line, discomfort and overcrowding, misunderstood announcements by railway staff and places with unpronounceable names (usually in Wales), romance, marriage and sex, women travelling alone, the class system and drunken passengers. Variations on these themes can be found throughout the history of the comic railway card, from about 1904 right up to the present day, an indication that certain aspects of the British character are unchangeable.

"IT'S NOT THE SIGNALS—IT'S THE WIND THAT'S AGAINST US!"

"SHAY GUARD, DOES THISH TRAIN CLAP AT STOPHAM JUNCTION?"

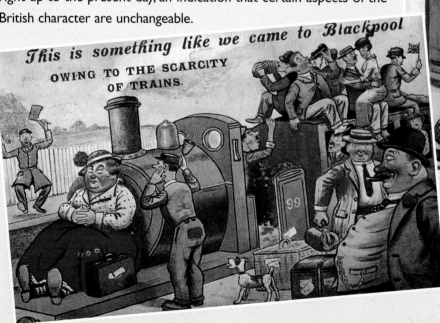

This is something like we came to Blackpool
OWING TO THE SCARCITY OF TRAINS.

These three cards illustrate three favourite railway themes: misunderstandings between staff and passengers, delay and discomfort, and drunken passengers. They cover a wide range of dates, from the 1950s at the top, 1927 above and 1917 to the left (with the message having a reference to the war). They all say 'having a fine time, weather good!'.

NEW PORTER: "IF THERE'S ANYONE 'ERE FOR THERE 'ERE IT IS!"

"ALL CHANGE!"
"I'VE CHANGED EVERYTHING BUT MY CHEMISE, GUARD. HAVE I TO CHANGE THAT AN' ALL?"

"SAWYER! SAWYER!!"
"ORL RIGHT, WE DON'T CARE IF YOU DID, WE WERE MARRIED THIS MORNING!"

FELLOW TRAVELLERS

"Hic, gimme a ticket pleash,"
"Very well" said the clerk "where do you wish to go?"
"You mindsh yer own buishness" says he,
"And gimme a ticket, and no pertinence,
I've got the money to pay, stand on me,"
Then the clerk gets annoyed, and says "hurry up, please,
What station do you want, don't talk rot,"
"What stationsh I want, why, I never thought of that,
I dunno, what stationsh have yer got?"

482

These cards explore the popular theme of misunderstandings between staff and passengers. The station with the longest name, in Anglesey, usually called LlanfairPG for short, has inspired several cards, this being a 1950s example. The postcard below, from 1911, features the marital theme with a ponderous pun (sadly, there never was a station called Sawyer). Confusion about changing trains is a familiar theme, represented in this 1927 card. Earliest, from 1904 and used as a birthday card, is the drunken ticket office exchange.

TOWN STATIONS

The major beneficiaries of the Victorian railway system in Britain were the small towns. Hitherto self-contained and relatively isolated, such places could now experience the benefits and pleasures of being part of an expanding national network. All over Britain, once the railways arrived, local industries thrived and people travelled. For this reason many towns became part of railway promotion schemes – some practical, some hopeless – into which large sums of local money were poured. These expressions of optimism are preserved in the names of countless early railway companies: the Leominster & Bromyard, the Callander & Oban, the Whitehaven, Cleator & Egremont, the Bishop's Stortford, Dunmow & Braintree, the Lewes & Uckfield, the Mellis & Eye, the Bideford, Westward Ho! & Appledore, the Llanidloes & Newtown and many, many more, all conceived as independent local ventures. Other towns gained their railway connection through the ambitions of the big companies, and in some cases inter-company rivalry meant that a place ended up with two, or even three stations, offering different routes and connections. Most welcomed the railway with open arms, but there were those that did not, conspiring with local landowners to keep it at a distance. Usually, however, local pride, a desire to be part of the railway revolution and the ever-expanding schemes of the big companies combined to put small towns on the railway map.

Crewkerne

▲ Cirencester, in Gloucestershire, had two stations and now has none. This is Cirencester Town, the GWR terminus at the end of the branch from Kemble, seen in 1959. It closed in 1964, but some of the buildings survive, indicating how well a local station could fit in with its surrounding architecture.

▶ Another partial survivor is Keswick, in Cumbria, though the line was closed in 1972. Here, the end is near and the flags are out as passengers board the local for Penrith. It was opened in 1865 by the Cockermouth, Keswick & Penrith Railway.

◀ Crewkerne station in Somerset was designed by Sir William Tite for the LSWR, following the pattern he established for that railway. Although reduced to one platform, it survives in reasonable condition and with adequate usage, despite being built a mile outside the town it serves.

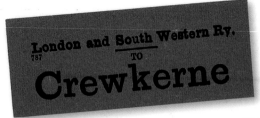

London and South Western Ry.

787

TO

Crewkerne

All this was to come to an end with World War I and then the closures began, prompted initially by the spread of the motor bus and the loss of goods traffic. During the 1960s small towns across the country lost their railways. Those that survived the axe were often much diminished through changing social patterns and the impact of private road transport.

Many town stations reflected the economic and architectural ambitions of their creators and were as a result buildings that made an impact in their own local environment. In many cases those that survive still echo the optimism, and the investment, that brought them into being. Others are lingering ghosts of former grandeur, unable to adapt to the demands of a changed world. After a spell in the doldrums, many small town stations are now enjoying better times. Passengers have returned, and station buildings have been restored and are now an important part of the national railway heritage. Many have been listed, including some that closed long ago. Others have been lost, or replaced by smaller, modern structures that are easier to maintain. Overall, however, the small town station is something special, an individual and sometimes eccentric reflection of local dreams and ambitions, and its continued existence is a vital legacy – and a barrier against the onward march of uniformity.

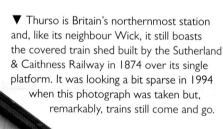

▼ Thurso is Britain's northernmost station and, like its neighbour Wick, it still boasts the covered train shed built by the Sutherland & Caithness Railway in 1874 over its single platform. It was looking a bit sparse in 1994 when this photograph was taken but, remarkably, trains still come and go.

▲ Workington Main was, as its name implies, the town's most important station. It was once a busy place, reflecting the local industrial wealth, but by the autumn of 1993 it was a decaying ghost, with long overgrown platforms far beyond the reach of the little railcars on the Cumbrian Coast line.

◄ Hawick, in the Scottish borders, benefited hugely from the arrival of the railway in 1849, and its textile industry flourished. The station was still busy in the Edwardian era, when this photograph was taken, but decline was steady from the 1930s and life finally came to an end in the 1960s.

Midland Railway. P.F. 70. E 2a.

HUNTINGDON

► This 1911 postcard shows the Great Northern's station at Huntingdon, in Cambridgeshire, built in 1850 to give a small town a mainline connection. Until 1969 it was known as Huntingdon North, to distinguish it from the Great Eastern's Huntingdon East.

WISH YOU WERE HERE!

EAST ANGLIA

*E*AST ANGLIA *was well served by railways, with a network built steadily from the 1840s. The main lines came first, linking London with the cities and the ports, but a remarkably diverse range of rural lines followed, particularly in north Norfolk. Tourist traffic was increasingly important on these lines from the 1880s and the railways played a major part in the development of east coast resorts. Postcards soon followed, featuring, as ever, stations great and small. In the Edwardian era these were vital documents, sent in huge numbers to arrange meetings and journey times or to tell friends or relatives about safe arrival in distant places.*

▶ *Clacton-on-Sea started out with a cottage-style station. It opened in 1882 and is seen here in about 1912, with an early motor bus outside. As the resort grew and flourished, the station became too small and it was rebuilt in the 1920s on a much bigger scale in a grand classical revival style.*

Railway Station, Clacton-on-Sea.

Dunmow. Railway Station.

◀ *This carefully posed photograph shows the once-substantial station at Dunmow, in Essex. Built by the Bishop's Stortford, Dunmow & Braintree Railway, it opened in 1869 as part of the Great Eastern's network. It is an interesting scene, showing plenty of detail, captured in about 1908. The line was closed to passengers in 1952.*

Spilsby, from the Railway Station.

◀ *Spilsby in Lincolnshire was at the end of a short branch line. Opened in 1868, the station was a very local affair. When this card was sent in 1905 it was still the centre of the community and was busy with goods of all kinds. The card was sent from Ida to her dad to say: 'we went to Spilsby gala last night and did not get home until twelve.'*

Thorpe Station, Norwich

▶ *Norwich once boasted four stations but today only Thorpe survives in use. It is a grand station, reminiscent of a French chateau. It was built in 1886. This card of about 1910 shows its then spacious setting and the famous pavilion-style roof. It also shows one of the trams that connected the station to the city centre.*

Trimingham Station, Norfolk.

◀ *Trimingham, a station on the coastal line linking Cromer and North Walsham, was part of the extensive Midland & Great Northern network in north Norfolk. Holiday traffic was the raison d'être for rural stations like this, so perhaps the elegant gentlemen with their bicycles were holidaying in the area. A novelty in about 1905, when this card was produced, was the coin-operated platform weighing machine.*

COUNTRY STATIONS

The steady expansion of the railway network across Britain from the 1830s made accessible thousands of small towns and villages that hitherto had been remote and largely isolated. Railways offered mobility to millions of people via the thousands of local stations built to serve almost every corner of the British Isles. Thus was born the typical country station, the most characteristic creation of the railway age yet remarkably diverse in style and structure. A country station was almost infinitely variable in size but usually had one or two platforms, a waiting room and ticket office, lavatories and a lamp room. Some had a stationmaster's office and facilities for parcels and left luggage. These passenger facilities were often sited within a multi-purpose building that could also be the stationmaster's house.

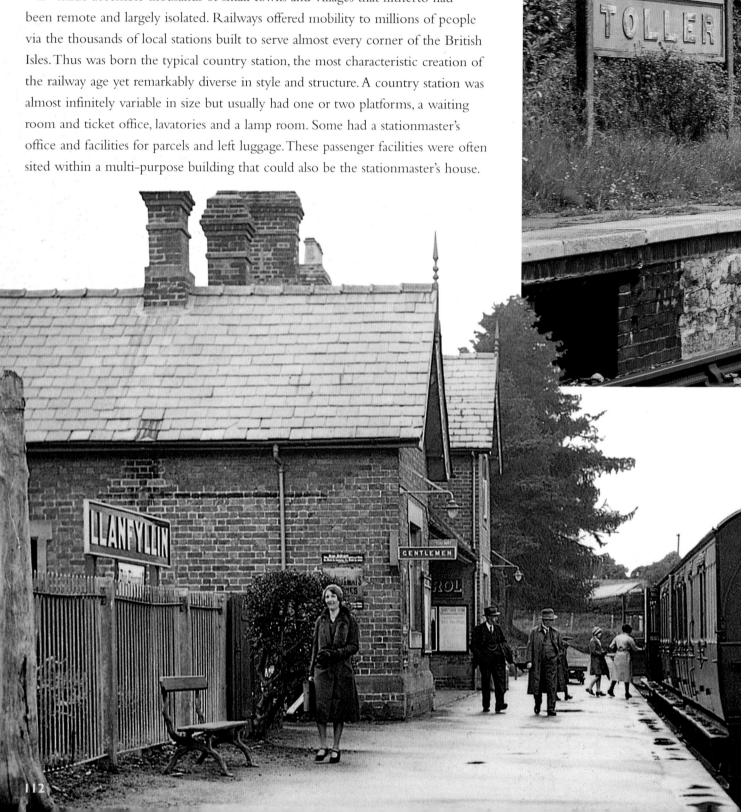

▼ In the summer of 1971 two passengers wait for the train at Toller, a station on the branch line from Maiden Newton to Bridport, in Dorset. Never busy, the small wooden station that served an extensive rural community is looking sad and uncared for. It closed in 1974.

◄ Llanfyllin was at the end of a branch line from Llanymynech, near Welshpool. In 1961 seven trains ran each way on weekdays, but the end was near. In 1932, as can be seen here, the train was at the heart of village life.

▲ A group of Edwardian children pose with the stationmaster at Cliddesden, a small station on the line between Basingstoke and Alton, in Hampshire. It closed to the public in 1932 but shot to stardom when it was used in the filming of the classic railway film *Oh, Mr Porter!* in 1937. Subsequently the line was dismantled and the rather basic, shed-like station was destroyed.

The platforms might be connected by a footbridge. In some cases there would be a number of associated structures, for example a signal box, a goods shed, a loading ramp, a water tower and, in country termini at the end of branch lines, a small engine shed. There could also be a network of sidings, to handle the goods traffic that kept the place alive.

The country station quickly became the heart of its community, a social centre for people travelling to and fro, and the point through which passed all supplies, materials and foodstuffs, all manufactured goods and agricultural produce. Newspapers and the mail came through the station and telegrams could be sent and received, making it a vital communications centre. Local shops were dependent on the railway, along with local businesses and farms. In its heyday the country station could and would handle everything, from livestock to bicycles, from building supplies to biscuits, from machinery to clothing and from coal to beer. Its buildings witnessed throughout the year the daily life of the people living in the town or village, young and old, in sickness and in health, and from its platforms children went to school, men and women went about their business or away on trips and visits, ladies went shopping and the young carried out their courting. The station staff were familiar figures in the local hierarchy with many living locally, and in a small community the stationmaster was a widely respected figure of considerable stature and importance.

Country stations were built in timber, brick or stone, their size and architectural

G.W.R.

Dursley

Mid. Rly.

▼ Leaning casually on his bicycle and framed by the extraordinary architecture of Dursley station, a young man, perhaps awaiting his girl, watches the train for Coaley Junction getting ready to depart in July 1947, headed by an elderly former Midland Railway tank locomotive.

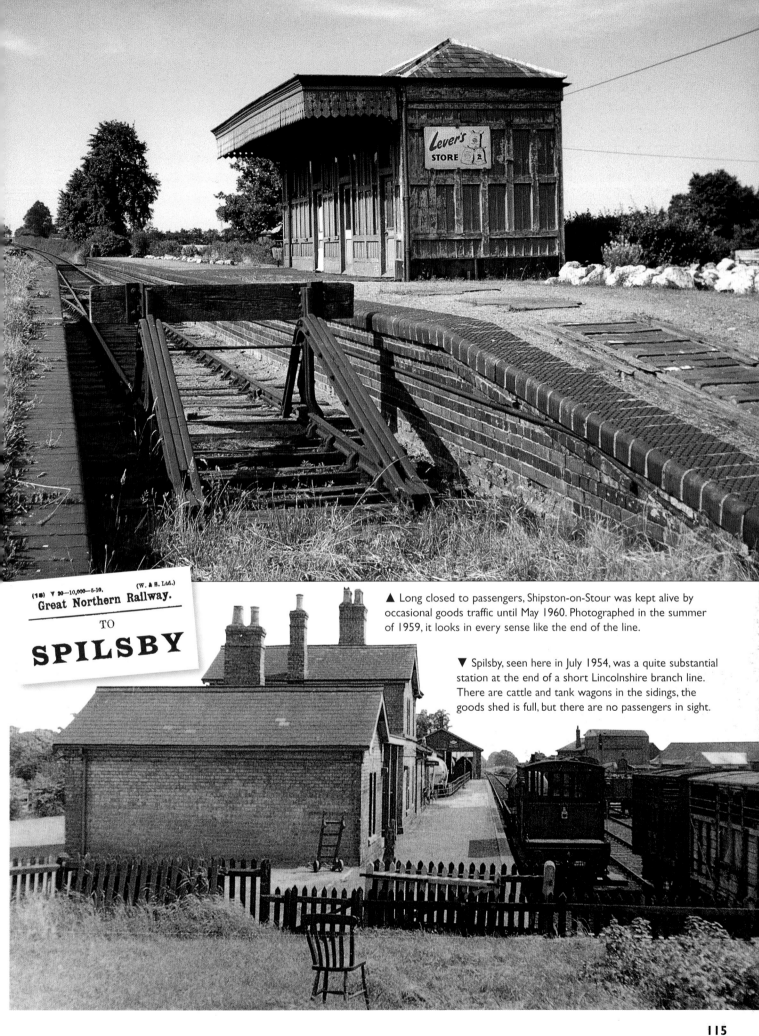

Great Northern Railway.

TO

SPILSBY

(18) ∀ 20—10,000—5-10. (W. & S. Ltd.)

▲ Long closed to passengers, Shipston-on-Stour was kept alive by occasional goods traffic until May 1960. Photographed in the summer of 1959, it looks in every sense like the end of the line.

▼ Spilsby, seen here in July 1954, was a quite substantial station at the end of a short Lincolnshire branch line. There are cattle and tank wagons in the sidings, the goods shed is full, but there are no passengers in sight.

Lever's STORE

complexity reflective of both the importance of the town or village and the wealth of the railway company that built them. Some single-storey buildings were little more than halts, while others were far more complex and significant, with plenty of decorative details often echoing vernacular styles and traditions. For about a century the country station thrived as an indispensable element in the social structure of rural Britain, enjoying as it did a monopoly in all the services it offered. However, competition from road transport became a major threat from the 1930s, initially from coaches and then increasingly from private cars. By the 1950s country railways, and thus country stations, were in serious decline, with many kept in business only by the goods and freight services they continued to offer. Facilities and staff were withdrawn and buildings were closed up or even demolished. When Dr Beeching published his report in 1963, he recommended

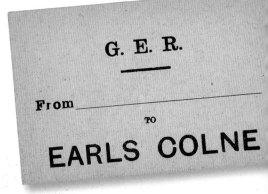

◄ In this perfect country railway scene, a push-pull train with a GWR pannier tank waits to depart from Marsh Mills station, in south Devon. It is 1961 and mothers and their children, in light summer clothes, have returned from a shopping trip to Plymouth. The driver waits, and the signalman watches from his window, ready to send the train away as soon as the passengers have safely crossed the tracks.

▼ Earls Colne was a typical country station on the rural East Anglian line from Haverhill to Chappel & Wakes Colne via Halstead. This carefully posed photograph, complete with the statutory children, shows the station in the Edwardian era. Judging by the photographer's position, and knowing the time it must have taken to set up the shot, trains were clearly not very frequent.

◀ Rural East Anglia was particularly well served by railways, the Victorians having built an extensive network that brought life to so many isolated communities. Typical was the line that went south from Swaffham through empty farmland to Roundham Junction and Thetford. Stow Bedon was one of the little villages on the line, yet the station, in local flint and brick, was comparatively substantial. Here, on a quiet, clear winter's day in the 1950s, two women and a child walk away from the platform. This line closed in 1964, along with many other East Anglian routes.

Goudhurst

the closure of over 2,000 stations, the majority of which were sited in small towns and villages. Some areas, notably rural Scotland and Wales, were particularly hard hit, losing not only local stations but entire routes. Hundreds of country stations were lost, along with their history and their long tradition of community service. The majority were demolished but there were many that survived, sold off and converted to domestic or business use. These can usually be readily identified and are often well cared-for, at the centre of rural communities increasingly devastated by the spread of road transport. It is an irony that the solution to the problem faced by so many small towns and villages could have been the country railway.

▼ Striking stone architecture, complete with stepped gables, a pretty canopy, a tidy little signal box and spectacular scenery, makes Dalmally a country station worth visiting. It is on the line from Crianlarich to Oban, to the east of Loch Awe. Handsome stations serving small communities are a feature of many of Scotland's rural routes.

▼ Bishops Waltham, seen here on a quiet day in 1959, was an extravagantly grand station at the end of a minor Hampshire branch line. The scale and richness of the architectural decoration seems out of place.

S.R. BISHOPS WALTHAM

▼ The Hawkhurst branch, in Kent, was notable for its very tall station buildings, far larger than the line would seem to justify. This is Goudhurst, on a quiet day in the early 1960s. A train waits to depart, a passenger wanders past, but otherwise the place seems to be deserted. A motorcycle is parked on the platform – perhaps the signalman, has left it there, ready for the end of his shift.

FLOODS AND SNOWSTORMS

RAILWAYS HAVE ALWAYS have been blighted by snow. Drifts block lines and derail trains, and even a minor fall can cause problems with signals and points and hinder staff movements, creating delays and cancellations. A number of serious accidents have been caused directly by snow, for example the collision at Abbots Ripton, near Huntingdon, in 1876. In severe winters, lines crossing rugged terrain have often been closed for days, while the notably bad winters of 1947 and 1963 resulted in weeks of disruption. More recently, in 1991, the railways became a national laughing stock when managers blamed delays on 'the wrong kind of snow'. Many lines, stations and other structures have also been damaged or destroyed by flooding. Swollen rivers frequently cause widespread inundations, while torrential rain and flash floods can cause landslides and destroy bridges, for example the Ness crossing, north of Inverness, swept away in 1989.

▲ Staff at St Bees on the Cumbrian Coast line near Whitehaven take a break from platform-clearing duties after a big snowfall in the 1890s. However, the drifts between the platforms will stop the trains running.

▶ In February 1971 the up Cornish Riviera Express, under the control of a class 47 diesel locomotive, passes through Midgham station, near Newbury, fighting its way towards Paddington in a violent snowstorm.

► It is the winter of 1947 and train services all over Britain face weeks of disruption. Drifting snow has brought traffic to a complete halt at Beaufort, a station in the Welsh Marches serving a mining community.

◄ Some areas are prone to regular flooding, for example parts of Somerset. Here, in about 1910 at Langport West on the Great Western line from Yeovil to Taunton, the track has become a river but, remarkably, the services are still operating and the crowds watch with interest the approaching train's bow wave.

TOWN AND COUNTRY
HALTS

The most basic, and in some ways the most appealing, type of station is the rural halt. These take the railways back to their infancy, when stations were just places where the trains stopped, places that lacked any facilities or amenities including even platforms. However, the halt is actually a later development, reflecting the increasing pressure on railway companies after World War I to compete with bus and tram services. There were, of course, always rather minimal or basic stations in remote regions, but the unstaffed halt is primarily a particular type, born out of this new kind of competition.

The appeal of the halt is its diversity, with seemingly endless varieties of both buildings and platforms. Halts were designed to be cheap to build and cheap to maintain, often consisting of little more than a rudimentary shelter, usually made of wood, and a single platform that was not infrequently well below than the doors of the train. There would be a name board, possibly a place for timetables

▲ Not to be confused with Shipton on the Paddington to Worcester line, Shipton-on-Cherwell Halt was the only intermediate station on the short Woodstock branch in Oxfordshire. Judging from this 1930s photograph, it was fairly inaccessible but well looked after and well lit. It also attracted its fair share of passengers. The bridge over the river Cherwell is just beyond the station.

◄ Two young women, perhaps going shopping in Aberystwyth, wait at Caradog Falls Halt as Manor class no. 7826 drifts in with a train from Carmarthen on 11 July 1964. With closure looming, the station is looking rather unkempt, though the GWR colours survive.

▲ Cold Harbour Halt, seen here on 15 June 1962, was the first stop east of Tiverton Junction on the Hemyock branch, in Devon. The basic wooden shelter and platform supported on old sleepers were typical of so many halts. Passenger traffic ceased in 1963.

SOUTHERN RAILWAY.

(8/45) (787)

FROM WATERLOO TO
IDMISTON HALT

and posters, and occasionally some form of lighting.

The shelters tended to look like garden sheds and were often scratch-built. Not unusual were shelters made from the bodies of retired railway vehicles. Corrugated iron was also used. Some companies did develop standard halt shelters that could be prefabricated in factories and assembled on site. The most famous of these was the GWR pagoda, assembled from a frame structure clad with corrugated iron and notable for the elegant curve to the roof. From the 1920s onwards, shelters, and indeed complete halt stations, were built from prefabricated cast-concrete sections made in factories that produced all kinds of railway buildings, structures and equipment, from goods sheds and footbridges to fence posts. Prefabricated concrete was also used for platforms. The earliest examples of platforms, however, were made from a variety of materials. A favourite was elderly sleepers, used for the platform itself as well as for the edging and for the structure. In other cases, the structure was made from old lengths of rail. Make do and mend, and minimum expenditure, were the guiding principles.

Some halts were built to serve military establishments, hospitals and other similar institutions; others were for use by workmen, and yet others were

▲ All over Britain there were halts built for limited use, for example by military camps or hospitals, or by workmen. Many were not listed in the timetables, and tended to be minimal in construction. Typical is Hardley Halt, on the branch to Fawley, in Hampshire, a workman's station in use from 1918 to 1965. It was built from a prefabricated concrete kit.

▲ A smart lady going shopping and a guard starting his shift watch the approaching train at Blaisdon Halt in south Gloucestershire on 20 November 1963. An old corrugated iron shelter and a rather ramshackle lighting system suggest decay, but new concrete sleepers have been laid.

▼ Ivatt no. 41291 draws its single carriage away from Combpyne en route for Axminster, in Devon. This most basic station, seen here in 1965, at the end of its life, actually had a station building away to the left of the photograph. For many years a camping coach inhabited the siding.

▲ Shoot Hill was a most basic station on that most basic railway, the Shropshire & Montgomeryshire, seen here soon after its opening in 1911. Virtually all its stations were halts, and it had an erratic existence until regular passenger traffic ceased in 1933. During World War II it was taken over by the War Department and then dismantled after 1947. The rather bizarre locomotive was no. 1, 'Gazelle', the pride of the fleet.

privately owned. Generally these were not in the timetable and so were used only by special trains or by trains stopping in response to prior arrangements. However, the vast majority of halt stations were listed in timetables and were included in scheduled stopping services. Many operated on a request-only basis, so passengers on the train had to inform the guard in advance if they wanted to get off, while passengers awaiting trains had to give clear hand signals to make them stop. Even today, many request stops survive in the network and operate on the same basis.

Halts are primarily in rural locations but there have always been some in towns and cities. These tended to be minor or subsidiary stations that saw only light or occasional traffic. One railway company, the GWR, had a kind of superior halt,

▲ The new station at Meadowhall, near Sheffield, boasts a particularly smart version of the modern steel and glass shelter. Many designs have been manufactured and used on lines all over Britain. Today the challenge to designers is not weather but vandalism.

◄ A famously unusual halt shelter is the octagonal one in timber at Duncraig, just east of Plockton on the Kyle of Lochalsh line. This station was known originally as Duncraig Platform, the nearest the Kyle line ever came to using the word halt.

◄ Another eccentric little railway was the Rye & Camber Tramway in Kent, whose 2-mile line opened in 1895. It was later extended to Camber Sands, where this rudimentary wooden terminus station was set right in the dunes. Described in the timetable as perfect for picnics, it was taken over by the Admiralty in 1939, and never reopened.

► The classic GWR pagoda station shelter is shown to perfection in this 1950s view of Nanstallon Halt, on the Cornish line between Wadebridge and Bodmin. This picture also shows a typical prefabricated concrete platform and name board, some smart lighting and a large garden roller, presumably for keeping the platform surface in order.

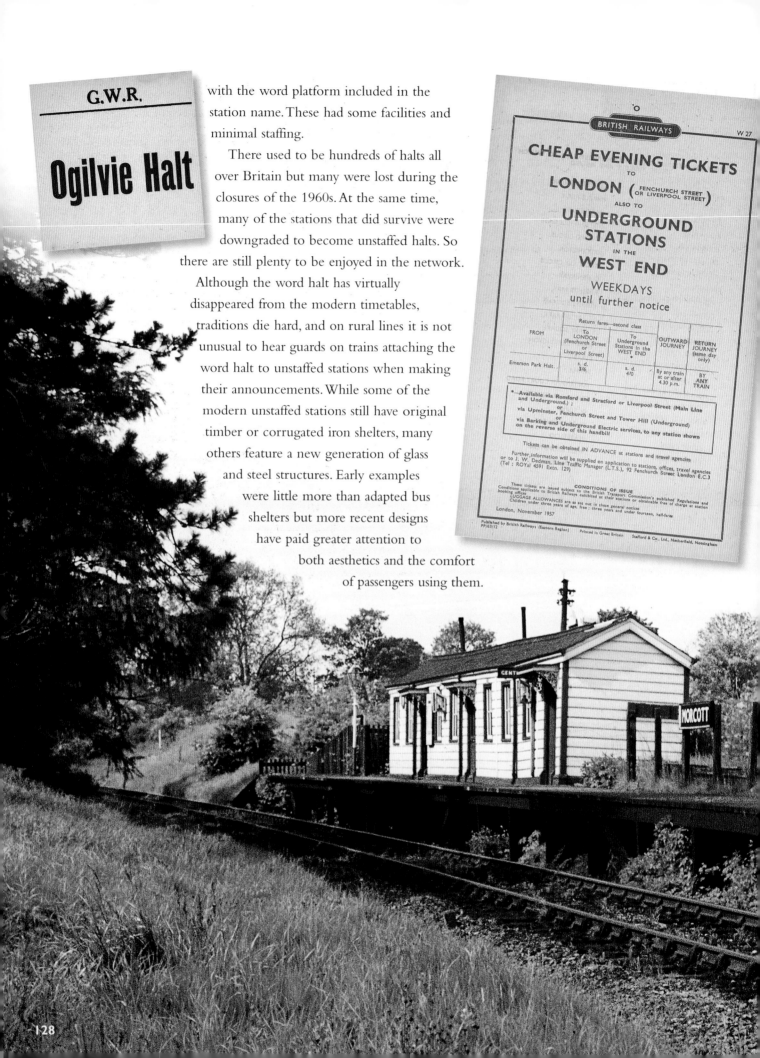

G.W.R.

Ogilvie Halt

with the word platform included in the station name. These had some facilities and minimal staffing.

There used to be hundreds of halts all over Britain but many were lost during the closures of the 1960s. At the same time, many of the stations that did survive were downgraded to become unstaffed halts. So there are still plenty to be enjoyed in the network. Although the word halt has virtually disappeared from the modern timetables, traditions die hard, and on rural lines it is not unusual to hear guards on trains attaching the word halt to unstaffed stations when making their announcements. While some of the modern unstaffed stations still have original timber or corrugated iron shelters, many others feature a new generation of glass and steel structures. Early examples were little more than adapted bus shelters but more recent designs have paid greater attention to both aesthetics and the comfort of passengers using them.

BRITISH RAILWAYS

W 27

CHEAP EVENING TICKETS
TO
LONDON (FENCHURCH STREET OR LIVERPOOL STREET)
ALSO TO
UNDERGROUND STATIONS
IN THE
WEST END
WEEKDAYS
until further notice

FROM	Return fares—second class		OUTWARD JOURNEY	RETURN JOURNEY (same day only)
	To LONDON (Fenchurch Street or Liverpool Street)	To Underground Stations in the WEST END *		
Emerson Park Halt	s. d. 3/6	s. d. 4/0	By any train at or after 4.30 p.m.	BY ANY TRAIN

*—Available via Romford and Stratford or Liverpool Street (Main Line and Underground.) ;
or
via Upminster, Fenchurch Street and Tower Hill (Underground)
or
via Barking and Underground Electric services, to any station shown on the reverse side of this handbill

Tickets can be obtained IN ADVANCE at stations and travel agencies

Further information will be supplied on application to stations, offices, travel agencies or to J. W. Dedman, Line Traffic Manager (L.T.S.), 92 Fenchurch Street London E.C.3 (Tel : ROYal 4591 Extn. 129)

CONDITIONS OF ISSUE
These tickets are issued subject to the British Transport Commission's published Regulations and Conditions applicable to British Railways exhibited at their stations or obtainable free of charge at station booking offices
LUGGAGE ALLOWANCES are as set out in those general notices
Children under three years of age, free : three years and under fourteen, half-fare

London, November 1957

Published by British Railways (Eastern Region)   Printed in Great Britain   Stafford & Co., Ltd., Netherfield, Nottingham
PP/63/12

◄ In this 1950s photograph of Whitlock's End Halt, south of Birmingham, the station seems to have met its end. The name board has collapsed, the platforms are looking rather ragged. However, the wooden shelter is in good order, indicating that, despite appearances to the contrary, it is still in use.

▼ An old NER class J69 tank locomotive no. 68616 and its equally ancient carriages pause at Feering Halt on 12 August 1950. This most basic station, whose shelter is formed from a long-abandoned wagon body, was just south of Kelvedon in Essex, on the Tollesbury branch.

◄ Emerson Park is today a commuter station on the link line between Romford and Upminster, in Essex. In 1963, when British Railways issued this handbill, it was still known as Emerson Park Halt and as such was a rare example of a halt being the starting point for special journeys.

▼ In 1966 Morcott was an old timber station, quietly fading away, between Seaton in Rutland and Stamford in Lincolnshire. Platform and track are overgrown, and the fencing has been removed, along with some of the signs – all indications that the trains have ceased to run. Closure came in July that year.

SMELLY & SMOKY

THE SPECTACLE of smoke and steam will always be associated with what many regard as the golden years of the railway. Yet the reality was often smelly and smoky, as well as spectacular in a noisy and dirty way. Recreated by preserved locomotives all over the world, much to the excitement of spectators and photographers, scenes such as those shown here were a daily feature of railway life in the steam age. The emission of large clouds of smoke and steam, particularly when locomotives were starting off a heavy train or working hard up an inclined track, was unpleasant for passengers and staff alike, but accepted as inevitable.

▲ With an impressive display of smoke and steam, a Q6 class locomotive makes its mark on Boldon Colliery station as it rushes through with a load of coal from Seaham for Tyneside power stations in the 1960s.

▶ This visitor to the North Yorkshire Moors preserved railway seems to be taking a deep draught of steam at Grosmont, perhaps reliving the railway experiences of his youth.

◀ This 1930s postcard shows a GWR Saint class locomotive, 'Saint Dunstan', hauling a Bristol express out of Paddington, amid great clouds of black smoke. The use of this image on a popular postcard shows how much such scenes were taken for granted.

▼ Even diesels can create clouds of evil-smelling smoke, often as a result of poor maintenance. In September 1975, class 52 'Western Gladiator' begins to emerge from its own smokescreen as it heads a Penzance train out of Exeter St David's.

JUNCTION STATIONS

Hundreds of stations all over Britain have at one time or another included the word Junction in their title, the term being used in its broadest sense to indicate a meeting point or divergence of lines. Perhaps the most famous example is Clapham Junction (actually in Battersea), in South London, which has claimed at various points to be the busiest station in Britain, or even in the world. At the other end of the scale are those remote junctions in the depth of the country, where a little-used branch line wanders away from a quiet main line. Most of these disappeared in the closures of the 1960s but they have left a lasting legacy of fond memories. Whether urban or rural, large or small, junctions have always added interest to the railway experience, inseparable as they are from the process of changing trains.

There are many types of junction. The earliest, associated with tramroads built to transport coal, stone and other bulk materials, was simply a separation of two tracks, effected by a primitive form of points. This type of junction has been used continuously from early days right up to the present time, though in increasingly more sophisticated and complex ways that involve large numbers of sets of points, diamond crossings, tunnels or flyovers. Another type was

▲ Wareham, in Dorset, was a classic junction station, though the junction itself was over a mile to the west. Here, in the 1960s, the Waterloo to Weymouth express, headed by Merchant Navy class locomotive 'United States Lines', pauses to allow passengers to change for the Swanage branch line train, waiting in the bay platform. Both trains are ignored by the men involved in the platform repairs.

◄ In 1964 a local freight from Presteigne, in Powys, hauled by an ancient tank engine, runs slowly past the long-closed station at Titley Junction. This remote spot was once the meeting place for four lines, two of which were branches, to Radnor and Presteigne.

► Polegate, in Sussex, was a complicated junction, as the tracks shown on this 1914 postcard indicate, yet only one line branched northwards away from the main route between Lewes and Eastbourne.

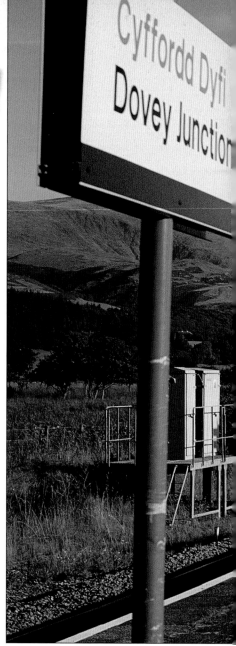

where two lines, perhaps built by separate companies, met end-to-end. The word Junction has also been used to describe crossings on a section of track from one line to another without any divergence of route.

Many junctions occur at places where there is no station, but they are nevertheless named for ease of identification. However, it was usual for a station to mark a junction, particularly if passengers changed trains there. In many cases such stations were initially isolated but their existence often encouraged the development of a local community. Sometimes junction stations carry the name of the place where they are located, however insignificant, and sometimes their name indicates the place that can be reached from there. Seaton Junction, in Devon, was an example of the latter, with the actual junction for the branch line being some miles away from Seaton itself. This could cause confusion for passengers, notably when a town had several stations. In the same part of the country, in neighbouring Somerset, there were once four stations that had Yeovil in the name – Town, Junction, Pen Mill and Hendford.

Junction stations could be linear, triangular or Y-shaped in their layout, and to some extent this determined the nature and style of the buildings in the station complex.

▲ Dovey Junction is a glorious spot, framed by hills and looking down the river valley towards the sea. Remarkably remote, it is a junction station that simply marks the meeting point of two routes and allows people to change trains. There is nothing apart from the platforms – and, for those who miss their connection, the view.

◀ At Barnstaple Junction, in Devon, seen here in the 1960s with a local departing towards Bideford, lines for Ilfracombe and Halwill Junction diverged either side of the signal box. The junction station, now the truncated end of the line from Exeter, is some way from the town centre, originally served by Town station.

▶ Dingwall was much enlarged by the Highland Railway after the opening of the line to Kyle of Lochalsh and the branch to Strathpeffer. The result was its attractive stone junction station, with a grand ridge-and-furrow canopy and a delicate iron footbridge.

CRASHES

AILWAY ACCIDENTS are as old as railways, and people have been killed by trains since the 18th century. The three main causes of accidents have been: technical failure of equipment, inadequate operational control, and human error. The first of these, with results ranging from exploding boilers to collapsing bridges, became steadily rarer as technology improved. The second, at its most common during the rapid growth of the network before the 1870s, was brought under better control by constant improvements in communications, signalling technology and vehicle braking. Human error, unfortunately, remains unpredictable and ever present, although modern technology, such as Automatic Train Protection, increasingly takes the decision-making and control out of human hands. In the early 1840s the government, mindful of public concern about the frequency of accidents and the lack of response from railway companies, introduced the first of a series of Parliamentary Acts that established an independent inspectorate to investigate all railway accidents and make recommendations in their reports. The worst accident in British railway history took place in Quintinshill, near Gretna Green, in 1915, involving five trains and 227 deaths. Human error was the cause but fires in the gaslit wooden carriages exacerbated the result.

▲ One of Britain's most mysterious accidents took place at Grantham, Lincolnshire, late on 19 September 1906. A train bound for Edinburgh, due to stop at Grantham, swept through the station at speed and was derailed. The dead included the train crew, so the cause was never established.

▼ On 10 November 1946 a permanent-way failure derailed the 4.45pm Newcastle to Kings Cross express at Marshmoor, in Hertfordshire.

BOAT TRAIN DISASTER AT SALISBURY.

▲ Postcard publishers were fascinated by train crashes. This one shows the wreck of the Plymouth to Waterloo boat train at Salisbury, following the crash late on 30 June 1906, This, which killed 28 people, was caused by the driver ignoring the 30mph speed limit through Salisbury station and going through at at least 60mph. The train derailed east of the station and crashed into a milk train. Amazingly the locomotive, shown here, was later driven away.

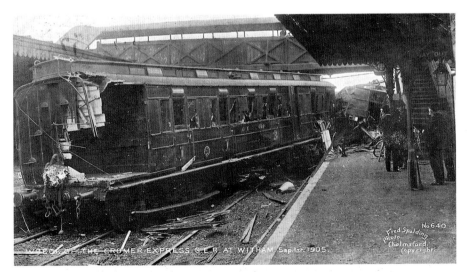

WRECK OF THE CROMER EXPRESS G.E.R. AT WITHAM Sep.1st 1905.

No.640
Fred Spalding
photo.
Chelmsford.
Copyright.

▲ On 1 September 1905 the 9.27am Liverpool Street to Cromer express was derailed at high speed at Witham, Essex, by a loose rail, the result of careless track maintenance. Parts of the station were demolished. This postcard, sent from Norwich just over two weeks later, makes no mention of the accident. However, it shows how quickly the cards could be issued.

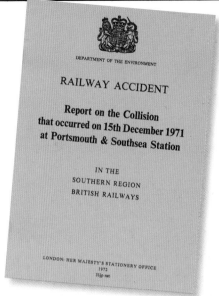

▲ Every accident, however minor, has to be fully investigated. This is the report into a minor collision at Portsmouth on 15 December 1971, caused by a driver passing at slow speed a red signal.

◄ Many accidents are minor and do not involve any loss of life or injuries. This Edwardian photograph shows some derailed wagons at Dawlish, in Devon.

IN THE MIDST OF LIFE WE ARE IN DEATH.

▲ One of the worst crashes in the Victorian era took place at Abergele, in north Wales, on 20 August 1868, when the Irish Mail collided at speed with some runaway goods wagons that included paraffin tankers. The public horror at the disaster inspired this memorial to the victims of the accident.

SEASIDE STATIONS

G.W.R.

Dawlish

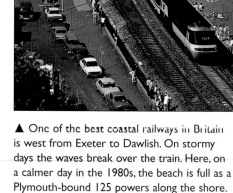

If preserved railways are included, there are over 220 stations in Britain that are on or very near to the sea. This is approximately ten per cent of all the stations in the country. For an island nation, these figures are perhaps not that surprising. However, what is more surprising is the way that they are spread evenly around the coast, with only parts of Scotland – as a result of both geography and the closures of the 1960s – being poorly served. Some of the earliest passenger railways in Britain, the Liverpool & Manchester, the Bodmin & Wadebridge and the Canterbury & Whitstable, were built to connect inland towns and cities with coastal harbours. By 1850, routes from London to Bristol, Dover, Folkestone, Brighton, Southampton, Newhaven, Portsmouth and Plymouth had been opened, along with lines to ports and harbours in many parts of England, Wales and Scotland. From this point the national network developed rapidly, and with it came many routes to the sea. This pattern of growth continued through the 19th century. By 1900 the map was nearly complete, leaving only a few lines to be finished in the early years of the 20th century. Among the last coastal stations were Padstow, reached in 1899, Mallaig in 1901, Lyme Regis and Lybster in 1903, and Camber Sands in 1908.

Trade was the primary driving force behind these lines, linking inland Britain with the ports and harbours around the coast. The efficient transport by train of raw materials and manufactured goods to and from the ports was a vital element in Britain's growth into the world's most powerful trading nation. Even little local harbours

▲ One of the best coastal railways in Britain is west from Exeter to Dawlish. On stormy days the waves break over the train. Here, on a calmer day in the 1980s, the beach is full as a Plymouth-bound 125 powers along the shore.

▼ Looe, in Cornwall, is the classic seaside station, with the line ending right by the harbour and estuary – a perfect finish to a lovely branch line journey of a kind now almost extinct in Britain.

▲ It is the end of the season and in September 1953 one of the last holiday trains bound for Wolverhampton sets off from Kingswear, headed by Hall class no. 4992 'Crosby Hall'. Today, this scene is regularly recreated by the preserved locomotives of the Paignton & Dartmouth Steam Railway.

could play their part, once they were railway connected. The major dock complexes built in the late Victorian era were designed for railway operation, for both general cargoes and specialized freight such as coal or fish, and this way of working did not change until the 1950s.

Goods were paramount in opening up the lines to the coast but passenger traffic increased in importance from the 1870s, thanks in part to increased wealth and leisure time and also to the advent of paid holidays. By the 1890s tourism was a major force and railways were instrumental in developing some of the principal seaside holiday regions in Britain, notably the south coast, East Anglia and the resorts of Lincolnshire and Yorkshire, south-west and north Wales, the Lancashire coast, western Scotland and the Highlands and Islands. Particularly important was the south-west of England, and it was the Great Western Railway that first called the south Devon coast the English Riviera. Railways built hotels and developed resorts on an unprecedented scale, and they used the most sophisticated marketing techniques to make sure the resorts were popular and their trains were full. As a result, generations grew up with the railway journey being an integral part of the seaside holiday experience. This pattern was maintained during the early decades of the 20th century and indeed was further encouraged by the proliferation of

GREAT WESTERN HOTEL AND GREAT WESTERN BEACH, NEWQUAY.

229

▲ The Great Western Railway was very keen on Newquay and did much to promote the resort, along with other Cornish destinations. Large sums of money were invested in buildings and structures, and the GWR made the most of its clifftop hotel and the beach it commanded which, as this card implies, was controlled by the railway as well.

◄ In July 1964 a French girl staying on the Isle of Wight sent this card to a friend in Paris; the weather was good, she was swimming, drawing and practising her English. At that point the island still had its own railway system, but most was about to be closed. Ryde Pier was for many the introduction to the island and its beaches and harbours, then accessible by train.

▼ Llandecwyn is a classic timber and corrugated iron halt with a wonderful sea view, typical of the Cambrian Coast line. Between Dovey and Pwllheli the sea is rarely out of sight and the train is often almost on the beach.

London Brighton & South Coast Railway.

South Hayling to
Ryde Pier

named expresses serving coastal destinations between the 1920s and the 1960s. These included boat trains such as the Golden Arrow and the Irish Mail, along with a great number of regular services, for example the Devon Belle, the Atlantic Coast Express, the Cambrian Coast Express, the Norfolkman, the Pines Express, the Scarborough Flyer, the Northern Belle, the Lord of the Isles and the Orcadian. Few named trains run today, and many of the lines to the coast were lost in the 1960s. However, there are still plenty of routes to be explored. It is also possible to take trains that follow the coast around much of Britain, offering spectacular scenery and memorable journeys in many parts of the country from the comfort of a railway carriage. Among the best are the main line from Exeter to Penzance, the Cornish branch lines, the Cambrian coast line from Dovey Junction to Pwllheli, the East Coast main line north of Durham, the Cumbrian Coast line from Carlisle to Arnside, and parts of the lines to Mallaig and Kyle of Lochalsh. Preserved and narrow gauge railways with coastal routes include the North Norfolk, the West Somerset and the Romney, Hythe & Dymchurch.

▲ One of the many great losses in scenic terms was the coastal route from Staithes to Whitby and Scarborough. Surviving traces of the route show how wonderful it was, and some of the grand stations, such as Stainton Dale, are now houses with magnificent views.

◄ Blackpool had three large stations, two of which were termini for holiday traffic. The scale of this business is shown by this 1920s aerial view showing the huge station and the extensive carriage sidings on the left.

P. F. 70.
R 2—25,000—8/07.

Midland Railway.

BLACKPOOL

► Wemyss Bay was developed as a Clyde steamer port by the Caledonian Railway, a successful venture that prompted the building of a new station in 1903. Its most famous feature is the circular glazed concourse, described by the sender of this card in 1934 as a 'huge conservatory with beautiful flowers'.

▼ The Cumbrian Coast line runs for much of its length along a dramatic shore. This is Braystones station seen from the beach in 1993, after it was damaged by fire.

STATION BUSINESS

THE MAIL

In 1830, the year of its opening, the Liverpool & Manchester Railway regularly carried mail on its trains. Other companies made similar arrangements with the Post Office and then in 1838 the Railways (Conveyance of Mails) Act was passed, enabling the postmaster general to require all railways to carry the mail. By 1842 at least 40 railway companies were involved in mail carrying and the first travelling post offices (TPOs) were in service. Dedicated mail trains ran from the mid-1850s, gradually replacing the postal carriages attached to passenger services. In 1882 posting boxes were fitted to carriages carrying mail sorters and these remained in use until the end of mail trains in 2004. In 1883 the railways began to carry parcels for the Post Office and in 1922 were still responsible for 90 per cent of this traffic. However, from the 1920s mail was increasingly carried by road, and later by air, leading to a gradual reduction in the number of dedicated mail trains.

A pile of mail bags was a familiar sight on station platforms all over Britain through much of the 20th century. The dedicated mail trains operated their regular schedules on the primary routes but local mail traffic still travelled in the guard's van on passenger trains. Collected at stations along the line, mail was delivered to the regional depot for onward distribution. As a result, many stations had mail-handling facilities and big stations had special platforms, areas or warehouses where the mail could be assembled and sorted. In country areas mail bags could be sent on complicated journeys, involving several

▲ Class J37 no. 64611 hauls its local freight train through Dunfermline Lower on a sunny evening in September 1966. In the foreground a pile of mail bags await collection – a familiar sight on platforms all over Britain at that time.

▼ The first dedicated mail trains ran westwards from Paddington in 1855. Here, on a summer's evening in June 2002, the tradition is maintained as the 19.30 TPO to Paddington prepares to leave Penzance.

changes of train before they reached the regional sorting office or the travelling post office. City stations had extensive mail-handling facilities, and in London several termini were linked by the Post Office's own underground railway, a narrow gauge system with fully automated trains. 1993 saw the launch of Railnet, a new nationwide mail-handling system based on a new terminal at Willesden, in north London, with specially built regional centres at stations in Bristol, Warrington, Doncaster, Newcastle and Glasgow. Railnet used a new generation of electric four-car mail trains for all routes except Bristol and the west of Britain, and container trains for the bulk transport of mail. However, the carriage of mail by train, along with the TPO service, ended in 2004.

▶ Big city stations had large areas dedicated to the handling of mail. This scene of orderly chaos was photographed at London Bridge in March 1990 as sorters, guided by place names hanging from the roof girders, shuffled the high-sided mail carts into their correct places for the receipt and despatch of mail bags. In the background mail vans wait. Activity is limited because it is the lunch break.

GOODS AND PARCELS

The early railways were quick to realize that there was money to be made from carrying parcels and in the 1840s some companies established local delivery networks. This traffic expanded rapidly, largely because the Post Office was not able to offer a comprehensive parcels service until the 1880s. Even that was dependent upon the railways for distribution to the regional sorting offices. The emergence of motor vans in the Edwardian era began to threaten the railway's monopoly of parcels traffic, but this competition did not become serious until the 1920s. The railways responded by setting up their own fleets of vans and lorries for local collection and distribution. After nationalization, the railways were initially able to hang on to much of the traffic as the British Transport Commission was responsible for both road and rail services.

The goods and parcels services looked after everything that travelled by train other than bulk cargoes and major freight. The parcels service,

▲ A large consignment of Walker's Scone Flour is loaded on to a local goods service in the 1890s. The exact location is unknown, but the North British open wagon offers a clue.

G. W. R. COLLECTED LUGGAGE.			(1413 C)
FROM			FOR STAMP
TO			
ON	RLY. VIA	STATION	

No. of Packages	No. of Passengers		Excess Charges to pay
	1st Class	3rd Class	

One of these labels to be affixed to each package.

350 pads, 100 lvs.—B.M. 60. 1947. (11) S.

▶ Panniers of strawberries wait to be loaded at Cheddar station while everyone stops to look at the camera. Perishable cargoes were collected from the station sidings, warehouses and loading bays for rapid onward transport.

which concerned goods and parcels that travelled in the guard's van on passenger trains, was the mainstay of the system. It encompassed anything portable, from livestock and perishables to supplies for shops and manufacturers, and until the closures of the 1960s it reached every corner of the network, literally keeping remote communities alive. The parcels service was universally popular, although the time spent loading and unloading at stations often caused delays. In addition, there was a nationwide pick–up goods service, whereby full or part loads were brought together in goods wagons in sidings and depots all over the country, taken to the local marshalling yard on a daily or weekly basis and then redistributed to the end user by rail and road delivery. Its smooth operation depended on the keeping of complex and elaborate records so that wagons and their contents could be tracked through the network.

▶ Red Star, the national rail express parcels service, was introduced in 1973. Though expensive, it was efficient and widely used, thanks to the receipt and despatch offices that were set up in passenger stations across the country. The service ended in 1991.

Red Star Timetable
FROM AND TO LONDON
11 May 1987 – 15 May 1988
NEW
≢
You've got a deadline
We've got the lifeline

▶ A typical local pick-up goods service pauses at Bromyard on the soon-to-be-closed rural line between Worcester and Leominster while some parcels are loaded and the driver has a chat. It is the summer of 1964 and the station garden seems a bit out of control – or perhaps, with closure imminent, the weeds are are being allowed to take over.

◀ Distracted momentarily by the camera, a young trainspotter, notebook in hand, makes the most of a busy scene at Carnforth, Lancashire, in June 1966. While Britannia no. 70011 'Hotspur' takes on water, station staff load a variety of packages, including perishables, into the parcels van of the down parcels express, a train that would run at the same speed as a passenger service.

ANIMALS

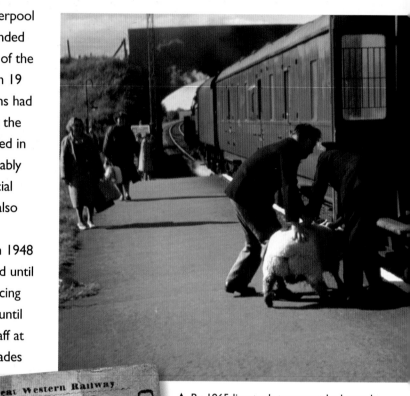

THE FIRST RAILWAY to carry livestock was the Liverpool & Manchester Railway, in 1831. The trade expanded rapidly, becoming by the 1860s one of the mainstays of the network. In 1914 the railways transported more than 19 million sheep, cattle and pigs, and nearly 2,500 stations had livestock handling facilities. Traffic diminished through the 20th century and the carriage of livestock finally ended in 1973. Other animal cargoes included horses, and notably racehorses, the transport of which continued in special vans into the 1960s. Large numbers of horses were also employed by the railways for haulage, transport and shunting duties. When British Railways was formed in 1948 it inherited over 9,000 horses, some of which worked until the 1960s. Smaller livestock included chickens and racing pigeons, the latter carried in huge quantities, at least until the 1970s, in special wagons for release by station staff at distant places. Dogs were frequent travellers, for decades needing their own tickets while cats and other small pets went free. And then there were the station pets, so many dogs, cats and tame birds kept by staff.

Great Western Railway
ONE DOG
(Value not exceeding £2.)
CHESTER   CHESTER
TO
WREXHAM
Carriage Paid 6d.
This Ticket must be given up on arrival
SEE BACK
SE 594 X   070

▲ By 1965 livestock transport had greatly diminished, but animals were still carried in the guard's van from time to time. At Bailey Gate, on the Somerset & Dorset line, station staff struggle to force a reluctant stud ram on to the train.

▲ Huge numbers of horses were employed by the railways for shunting duties, usually in country goods yards and small dock yards where locomotives were not always available. In these circumstances, the quickest and cheapest way to shunt single wagons was to use horsepower. This Edwardian view shows a more unusual sight, a horse being used to shunt a passenger coach in a large city station, in this case Lincoln.

IN MEMORY OF THE DOG PRINCE DIED 1898 AGED

▲ It is a quiet day at Talybont-on-Usk in the summer of 1962 and the station is deserted – except for a cow that has decided to take a walk along the platform after escaping, presumably, from the station's cattle pens.

◄ Station pets often enjoyed long lives, thanks to constant indulgence from staff and passengers. In death they were much lamented and well treated, as indicated by these pet graves at Talyllyn Junction.

▲ Stations all over Britain had resident pets, usually cats or dogs. Here, staff at a small station pose for the camera: while the stationmaster hangs on to his cigar, one of his staff holds the pet mongrel.

THE RAILWAY HOTEL

Railways and hotels grew up alongside each other and were mutually interdependent. The first hotel built by a railway company opened at Euston in London in 1839, and from this point the acquisition, building and management of hotels become a significant part of railway business. Eventually all London termini with the exception of Fenchurch Street, Blackfriars and, surprisingly, Waterloo boasted a hotel, while equally impressive structures were to be found in Birmingham, Manchester, Liverpool, Leeds, Glasgow, Edinburgh and elsewhere. In some large cities served by several railway companies there were competing hotels. Major architects were involved, for example E M Barry at Charing Cross in London, Alfred Waterhouse at the North Western in Liverpool and George Gilbert Scott at St Pancras. Scott's Midland Grand Hotel is now one of the landmarks of London and its Gothic splendour is widely seen as the epitome of railway age architecture.

Although associated primarily with major towns and cities, railway hotels were soon to be found in ports, notably at Holyhead, Dover and Parkeston Quay, and provincial towns. Later, with the spread of leisure travel, railway hotels took their place in the development of seaside, sporting and country resorts. One of the earliest seaside hotels was the Zetland, built by the Stockton & Darlington at the developing resort of Saltburn. Later, railway-owned golf hotels became popular, especially in Scotland, with famous examples at Turnberry, Gleneagles and Cruden Bay. At first conservative and restrained in style, hotel architecture became more flamboyant and extravagant as the century progressed and as the ambitions, power and wealth of railway companies increased.

▲ The Glasgow & South Western was an adventurous company with interests in coal and tourism. It owned a number of hotels, including the famous golf hotel at Turnberry, and promoted them in an attractive way.

◄ The LNWR's Queens Hotel at Birmingham New Street was opened in 1854. Built in a formal classical style, it echoed the architecture favoured by the North Western's predecessor, the London & Birmingham, creators of London's Euston and Birmingham's Curzon Street stations.

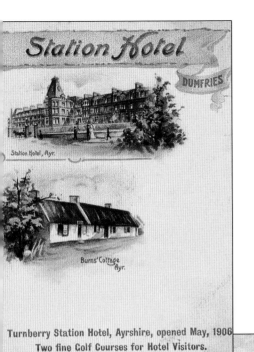

Station Hotel

DUMFRIES

Station Hotel, Ayr.

Burns' Cottage, Ayr.

Turnberry Station Hotel, Ayrshire, opened May, 1906
Two fine Golf Courses for Hotel Visitors.

LNER

PASSENGERS FROM LONDON TO EDINBURGH (Waverley Station), via THE EAST COAST ROUTE DEPART FROM KING'S CROSS STATION, AND BY THE MIDLAND RAILWAY ROUTE FROM ST. PANCRAS STATION

NORTH BRITISH STATION HOTEL

TELEPHONES:
CENTRAL
8966 to 8972

TELEGRAMS:
"BRITISH"
EDINBURGH

EDINBURGH.

THE HOTEL IS IN DIRECT COMMUNICATION WITH WAVERLEY STATION BY ELECTRIC LIFTS, AND THE HOTEL PORTERS ATTEND THE ARRIVAL OF ALL TRAINS.
ALL COMMUNICATIONS TO BE ADDRESSED TO THE HOTEL "MANAGER."

McC. & Co. Ltd.

▲ The North British Railway opened its grand hotel overlooking Edinburgh's Waverley station in 1902. The massive ten-storey stone structure was dominated by its great clock tower, one of Edinburgh's best-loved landmarks. This label, a typical railway hotel souvenir, dates from the LNER era.

◄ The prosperity of the Furness Railway in Cumbria was closely associated with the steel industry. When this trade declined in the 1880s, the railway switched to the promotion of tourism and enjoyed a new lease of life. The country-house style Furness Abbey Hotel dates from this period.

FURNESS ABBEY HOTEL.   FURNESS ABBEY STATION.

◄ Hull's Royal Station Hotel, completed in 1851, was one of the first to be built across the station concourse facing the platforms, a layout that soon became standard. British Transport Hotels was formed in 1962 to manage the remaining 37 railway hotels, and it survived until the early 1980s, when everything was privatized. This brochure dates from the 1970s.

► The Wyncliff Hotel, originally a private house, was acquired by the Great Western in 1898. Renamed The Fishguard Bay, it was extensively enlarged to serve the Irish trade in 1906. This card, dating from that period, shows its woodland setting away from the railway.

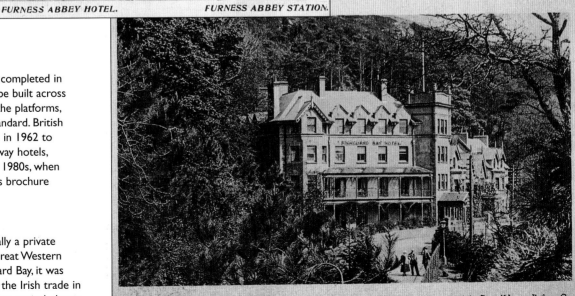

THE FISHGUARD BAY HOTEL.   *Under the management of the Great Western Railway Co*

The heyday of the railway hotel was probably at the end of the Victorian era, and in 1901 there were 61. In the 1920s and 1930s some hotels were closed but others were renovated in a smart Art Deco style. Best known of these was the widely promoted and highly fashionable Midland at Morecambe, designed by Oliver Hill in 1930. The hotels were separated from railway ownership in 1948 but came back under railway control in 1962 as British Transport Hotels, only to be sold completely in the early 1980s.

In architectural terms the railway hotel was the perfect reflection of Victorian ambition and extravagance. Classical, Gothic, Renaissance and French styles were favoured for the exteriors, and these were generally echoed by the interiors, which became more lavish as the century progressed. With their combinations of modern facilities and exciting decor and fittings, these hotels existed in a highly competitive environment, vying to attract custom. Huge and impressive dining rooms, lounges and public spaces were regularly renovated in the latest styles, while equally important were special features such as theatres, conference rooms and gardens. A remarkable example of this was the roof garden on top of the Midland Hotel in Manchester, which offered fine views across the city – weather permitting. Indeed, the Midland was famous for its hotels, the best known being the Grand at London's St Pancras station, which opened in 1873. Closure at an early date and subsequent use as offices enabled the original interiors to survive. Now being fully restored, these offer a unique insight into the glorious and rich extravagance of the Victorian railway hotel. At the end of the 19th century styles became more informal, with echoes of Arts & Crafts and Art Nouveau, and then in the 1920s and 1930s came modernism and Art Deco.

Midland Hotel, Manchester Roof Garden.

North Western Hotel, Liverpool. — New Grill Room, open to non-residents.

YORK, ROYAL STATION HOTEL. THE LOUNGE

▲ Liverpool's first railway hotel was the North Western and its dominant position remained unchallenged until the Midland railway took over and extensively rebuilt the Adelphi in the Edwardian era. This prompted a major updating of the North Western by the LNWR, illustrated in this card.

◄ York's Royal Station Hotel was opened in 1878. Extended in 1896, it had been lavishly refitted by the time this card was issued in about 1914. By then it boasted electric light and an electric lift, a motor garage, a typewriting room and 'one of the handsomest reading rooms in the kingdom'.

▲ Although a relatively late arrival on the scene, Manchester's Midland Hotel was one of the most spectacular. Its facilities included an 800-seat theatre and the roof garden shown on this card. It opened in 1903.

▲▶ The Midland Grand at London St Pancras, designed by Gilbert Scott and opened in 1873, was the greatest and most lavish railway hotel in Britain. Today, its spiky Gothic exterior is the icon of the railway age. More remarkable is the survival of its glorious interior, now under restoration.

WHY DID WE GO THERE?

LANDUDNO barely existed when the railway from Chester to Holyhead was opened in 1850 but the splendid qualities of the bay beneath the Great Orme were soon appreciated. A branch was built to the rapidly expanding resort, which soon became one of the smartest and most popular in north Wales. In the 1860s a line south to Betws-y-Coed opened up the delights of the Conwy valley and Snowdonia to visitors already able to enjoy the coastline and history of north Wales.

L. & N. W. RY.
Llandudno

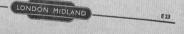

PLEASE RETAIN THIS PROGRAMME FOR REFERENCE

PROGRAMME
OF
ORDINARY RETURN TICKETS
TO
LLANDUDNO
AND
MENAI BRIDGE
VIA LIVERPOOL AND THE LIVERPOOL AND NORTH WALES S.S. CO.'S STEAMERS
WEATHER AND OTHER CIRCUMSTANCES PERMITTING

WEEKDAYS
th June to 10th September 1960

SUNDAYS
June to 11th September 1960
where train service permits

LONDON MIDLAND   E 23

LLANDUDNO BAY

▲ Llandudno's setting, on the wide curving bay between the Great and the Little Orme, is magnificent, and it was this that made the town a premier resort once the railway had arrived. Unlike many resorts on Wales's northern coast, Llandudno was able to be both popular and smart.

Love-Making in Wales.
REALIZATION

▶ This 1911 card reflects the Edwardian revival of interest in the traditional symbols of Welsh culture, including Welsh girls.

Something to SING about from SNOWDON SUMMIT

TRAIN LEAVING SNOWDON SUMMIT.

SNOWDON SUMMIT.

W. 3837

◀ No visit to north Wales was complete without a trip on the Snowdon Mountain Railway, though the route by train from Llandudno was rather circuitous. Betty, who sent this bizarre card in 1953, did the usual thing: train up, walk down.

▶ The LNWR published many cards in the Edwardian era to promote its north Wales services. This one, showing Conwy castle and Stephenson's remarkable railway bridge, was sent in May 1906 from London to Bradford. The writer says, intriguingly: 'Just off to the House of Commons.'

◀ Joint rail and ship excursions were always popular. This 1960 handbill advertises trips by train to Liverpool and thence by steamer to Llandudno and Menai Bridge, Return was by the same route, within three months.

Conway Castle

The Dingle Colwyn Bay.

◀ In 1906, when this card was sent, Colwyn Bay was still a quiet place, offering both seaside and rural walks inland. It was soon to develop into north Wales's largest resort, with a promenade 3 miles long.

ON THE ROAD

BRITISH RAILWAYS

SPECIAL ROAD SERVICES
BETWEEN
CAMBORNE/REDRUTH
AND
HELSTON (Cornwall)
ON
SATURDAYS ONLY—JUNE 22nd to SEPTEMBER 7th, inclusive, 1963

ON SATURDAYS ONLY during the above period special road services will operate from and to CAMBORNE station for the exclusive use of passengers holding through single and ordinary return tickets to HELSTON via Camborne. One special road service will operate similarly on these SATURDAYS in each direction between REDRUTH and HELSTON to connect with the "Cornish Riviera" Express (From Paddington: Redruth arrive 5.3 p.m.; To Paddington: Redruth depart 10.42 a.m.).

Details of the timetable for these special buses are shown overleaf.

PROVISION WILL BE MADE ON THE SPECIAL BUSES FOR PASSENGERS' ACCOMPANIED LUGGAGE

Passengers in possession of through rail tickets to Helston, arriving at Camborne or Redruth stations on the SATURDAYS referred to at times not covered by the special bus service will have their tickets honoured on the Western National Omnibus Company's existing stage carriage services—heavy luggage NOT conveyed—and should travel as under:

Camborne—Helston by Western National Omnibus Company Service No. 30.
Redruth—Helston by Western National Omnibus Company Service No. 31.

All passengers travelling beyond Plymouth from Camborne and Redruth by certain trains on Saturdays during the Summer Train Service are required to obtain a Special REGULATION TICKET, issued without charge, which ensures a seat on the train.

Regulation Tickets can be obtained in advance at any station or ticket agency on production of a valid rail ticket to cover the journey not later than three weeks prior to date of travel after which Regulation Tickets may be obtained on personal application at HELSTON, CAMBORNE or REDRUTH railway stations.

Further details of the special Seat Regulation Arrangements from West Cornwall Stations can be obtained from stations or ticket agencies.

Facilities are available at Helston station to deal with parcels traffic, including "Passengers' Luggage in Advance" arrangements, and the issue of rail tickets.

SEND YOUR LUGGAGE IN ADVANCE

R1417   S. E. RAYMOND, General Manager.

Printed by Latimer, Trend & Co. Ltd., Plymouth

Rivalry between road and rail has been ever-present. In their first decades the railways, offering faster and cheaper services, destroyed piecemeal a national network of horse-drawn transport for both goods and passengers. Most of the major carriers had disappeared by the 1850s and those that survived were often bought into railway ownership. As things settled down, a form of integration developed between road and rail. Short-distance road transport flourished, providing links to and from stations as well as local delivery and collection services. Initially these were operated by independent carriers but soon the railways began to operate their own fleets of horse-drawn road vehicles, and by 1900 well over a million horses were at work hauling goods and passengers on the roads of Britain. Only a fraction of these actually worked for railway companies but when British Railways was formed in 1948 over 9,000 horses were still in harness, along with over 25,000 horse-drawn vehicles. By the 1890s road vehicles were competing more efficiently over short distances, thanks to the development of steam and electric tramways and steam lorries. However, the real impact of road transport was not felt until the 1920s,

▲ The first buses operated by the GWR were run in connection with the Helston branch in Cornwall. This 1963 handbill shows that this habit lived on, with special summer Saturday buses running between Camborne/Redruth and Helston. The Helston branch from Gwinnear Road had closed to passengers the previous November.

▼ First developed in the early 1930s for use in difficult spaces and narrow city streets, the Scammell Mechanical Horse became the best-known railway vehicle, with over 15,000 in service between the 1930s and the 1960s. This preserved example was on show at the site of Clare station, in Suffolk, in 2004.

HOUSEHOLD REMOVALS BY ROAD-RAIL CONTAINER

The quickest and safest way

From every point of view the best way of having your furniture moved is by Road-Rail Container. The job is done without hitch or delay and you have everything straight in your new home in the shortest time possible. Road-Rail Containers are safest too—risk of breakage or loss is reduced to an absolute minimum. As for the cost, you'll be surprised how cheaply the Railways can do it.

EVERYTHING IS DONE FOR YOU

The Railways' Household Removal Service carries out the whole of the job, from start to finish. You need not worry about anything. The Road-Rail Container is brought to your door, all your household goods are carefully packed and taken direct by road and rail to your new home, where the packers place the furniture according to your instructions.

Throughout the journey nothing whatever is touched. Another big point—all members of your household get 33⅓% off the rail fare to the new home town, thus reducing still further your removal costs.

FREE ESTIMATES. The British Railways' Household Removal Service is the biggest removal organisation in the country. Estimates are supplied free of charge. Full details from any Railway Station or Enquiry Office.

BRITISH RAILWAYS' HOUSEHOLD REMOVAL SERVICE
The largest removal organisation in the country.

G·W·R LMS L·N·E·R S·R

SAY YOU SAW IT IN "THE RAILWAY GAZETTE"

▲ Advertisements in *The Railway Gazette* in 1935, with drawings by Frank Newbold, show the Big Four working together to promote road delivery services and the new road-rail container. They were marketed under the name British Railways long before nationalization.

▲ Somewhere in Somerset in August 1961 a British Railways lorry delivers luggage and equipment to a Girl Guides' summer camp. Apparently, having mislaid everything for five days, during which time the Guides no doubt coped manfully, British Railways were doing their best to make amends.

▼ Railway companies operated large fleets of motor vehicles for construction, maintenance and other activities related directly to the operation of the network. This 1930s photograph shows a brand new six-wheel tipper truck outside the Karrier works, ready for delivery to the LMS.

◄ Familiar to the many owners of Dinky toy models in Midland Region maroon, the British Railways horsebox was a successful railway vehicle during the 1950s, a reflection of the fact that racehorse traffic was still considerable at that time. There were dedicated services to and from courses with rail connections, and fleets of horseboxes to transport animals to courses not connected directly to the rail network.

▼ Issued by the LNWR in 1905, this card shows one of the horse-drawn family omnibuses operated by that company. These vehicles were designed to offer families personal transport along with all their possessions, including bicycles, between home and station.

SINGLE HORSE FAMILY OMNIBUS.

▲ Railways often worked with bus companies to offer excursions to places not linked to the network. This 1963 handbill promotes a combined rail and road trip to Dovedale.

◄ Railway companies began to operate their own motor bus services in the Edwardian era. This 1914 postcard shows a smart GWR example in service in Devon.

► Though never a railway vehicle in the strictest sense, the taxi has always been a vital part of the railway infrastructure, from Victorian hansom cabs onwards. This is the taxi rank at London's Euston on a day in 1947 when trade was a bit slow.

by which time motor buses and lorries were coming into service in large numbers. Private car usage also increased but it was the developing network of motor bus services, especially in rural areas, that badly affected the railways' dominance of short distance traffic. The railways responded by rationalizing services, cutting costs and running their own bus fleets. They also bought out some of the major freight carriers, notably Pickfords and Carter Paterson. After World War II, the railways began to lose the battle with road transport. This was due partly to the dramatic increase in car ownership (from 2 million in 1950 to 20 million in 1990), partly to the introduction of larger, more efficient lorries, and partly to a lack of government support. However, the railways never gave up and there were many innovations, including door-to-door container services, the development of dedicated and highly manoeuvrable delivery vehicles such as the Scammell Mechanical Horse, the use of specialized road vehicles like horseboxes, and the greater emphasis on integrated road and rail services using high-speed container liner train networks, developed in the 1960s and marketed under names such as Speedfreight and Freightliner. By the early 1980s Freightliner trains were carrying nearly a million containers a year.

▲ The railways employed thousands of horses for many tasks, from deliveries to shunting, and the last ones did not retire until 1967. However, from the 1920s onwards a variety of mechanical versions were developed. Here, in the 1950s a railway horse is introduced to his motorized replacement.

WISH YOU WERE HERE!
WALES

CONSIDERING THE NATURE of the landscape and the relatively small size of its population, Wales was remarkably well served by railways, both standard and narrow gauge. Freight was the inspiration for many of the lines but, by the era of the postcard, leisure and holiday traffic had become as important. As a result, postcard photographers were hard at work in the decade before World War I, capturing images at stations great and small all over the principality. Now that so many of the lines have closed, along with their stations, these cards provide an invaluable record of railway life in Wales, and are often all that remains of it .

▶ Llandrindod Wells lingers on today on the little-used Heart of Wales line. However, at its heyday in the Edwardian era, it was on an express route from London's Euston station, as this official card issued by the LNWR indicates. Such cards were issued by railway companies to encourage traffic, particularly on the new holiday routes. As a famous spa town at that time, Llandrindod Wells received thousands of visitors by train.

EUSTON EXPRESS AT LLANDRINDOD WELLS STATION
(L. & N. W. RAILWAY.)

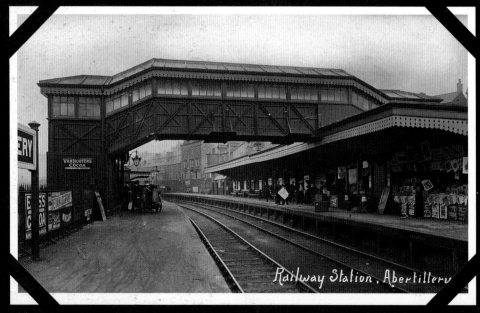

Railway Station, Abertillery

◀ Set on one of the dense networks of lines that filled the valleys north of Cardiff and Newport, Abertillery was a substantial station, complete with bookstall. Cards of this era give a clear idea of how important a role the railway played in its heyday.

This word 'Guide a...
...con gra. ...rioli.

◄ Posted in 1911 by a nanny away on holiday, this card shows Tan-y-Bwlch station, on the Festiniog Railway in north Wales. Slate wagons reveal the line's raison d'être, but by this date holiday traffic was taking over. Nanny wrote to her two charges, the Goddard brothers: 'Here is a picture of the toy railway. I do wonder what you will think of the funny little engine.'

► Following a huge increase in holiday traffic, Prestatyn station was completely rebuilt in 1897. This Edwardian card shows the station about ten years later, bustling with holiday activity: ladies in hats and bright dresses, people looking out of crowded excursion trains. After careful restoration in the 1980s, the station still looks like this.

STATION PRESTATYN.

TONYREFAIL

◄ Another valley line in south Wales was the short branch to Clydach, north of Llantrisant, built largely for the coal traffic. Tonyrefail was one of two intermediate stations. The photographer would have struggled to find somewhere more obscure but he has managed to persuade someone to pose for him. Sales for postcards like this were minimal, so they are rare today.

THE BOOKING OFFICE

In its infancy, railway ticketing was a complicated and time-consuming process involving handwritten slips torn from receipt books – hence the origin of the term booking office. However, this system was open to abuse and was inadequate for record-keeping. These problems came to the attention of Thomas Edmundson, a stationmaster working for the Newcastle & Carlisle Railway, and he developed a system of standardized, serially numbered, cardboard tickets with pre-printed destinations; the tickets could be mechanically dated when issued. They had three functions: to act as a receipt for the passenger's fare, to authorize a specific journey on a specific date, and to ensure that the railway company received all the money it was due (serial numbering meant that clerks had to account for every ticket). Edmundson moved to the Manchester & Leeds Railway in 1839 and that company quickly adopted his system over all its routes. Two years later he left, to set up with his son his own ticket business. From the 1840s the Edmundson system was adopted by railway companies all over Britain, with Edmundson receiving a royalty. In principle, this system remained in use throughout the British railway

▲ The size of the Edmundson ticket was standard, but each company had its own style. These Edwardian tickets show the key features, the printed numbers and dates.

▲ Stocks of old tickets often lasted for years. Here, in 1952, British Railways were still using up stocks of pre-nationalization GWR weekly season tickets.

◀ A ticket office at a large station was a busy place, with clerks working shifts. This BR photograph shows Southend Victoria in August 1961, with the walls still filled with racks of Edmundson tickets for every available destination and type of use.

▼ In the early days, tickets were sold at pubs and hotels. In some small stations, such as Farrington Gurney, near Radstock, this habit lingered on when the office – as often happened – was closed. Perhaps the dog needs a ticket.

◀ The barrier, seen here at Loughborough Midland in the 1920s, has always been a vital element in the process of ticket checking and control. Today, it is done with electronic gates and tickets with magnetic strips.

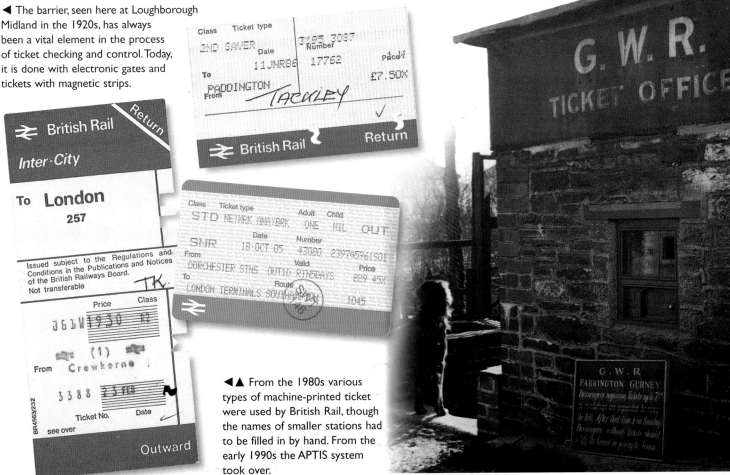

◀▲ From the 1980s various types of machine-printed ticket were used by British Rail, though the names of smaller stations had to be filled in by hand. From the early 1990s the APTIS system took over.

network until 1990, when the standard green, pre-printed cardboard ticket finally disappeared. While green dominated the 20th century, it was by no means the only colour. In the pre-Grouping era all colours were used, with variations from company to company and to denote different classes and different types of ticket – single or return, child, workman, military, excursion, platform, dog, cycle and so on. The recording of each ticket and its number was a heavy burden on the booking clerk. Despite this, and despite early attempts at improving the ticket-selling process, including coin-operated ticket machines, British Railways did not develop a system that printed tickets at the point of sale until the 1950s. This was brought into wider use in the 1960s, but still Edmundson survived in many parts of the network. It was the computer that finally changed the 150-year-old system when, after trials with various technologies, British Rail introduced APTIS (All Purpose Ticket Issuing System), whereby all ticket-selling machines are linked to a central computer. A portable version, SPORTIS, is used by guards issuing tickets on trains.

Technology apart, the booking or ticket office is still the most unchanged part of the station. Passengers still wait in queues to be served by a clerk behind a window, exactly as they did in the 1840s. There have been many variations in style and structure, and sometimes there were separate offices or windows for different classes or railway companies. At some big stations there could be up to six booking offices, and passengers needed to know both their place and their railway geography. Today, ticket offices are travel centres, and railways encourage online and advance booking – but it will take many years before the old Victorian habit of turning up, buying a ticket and getting on the train is finally broken.

▲ Platform tickets are largely a thing of the past, thanks to computers and the electronic barrier. However, modern examples can still be found.

▲ Many preserved railways, as part of their period re-creation, continue to use Edmundson tickets, both for journeys and for the platform, though these are often souvenirs.

▲ The clerks in the booking office had many responsibilities beyond selling tickets, including taking seat reservations and applying them to the right train.

▲ Large stations had separate luggage offices but on smaller ones the booking office clerks also had to organize passengers' luggage, much of which travelled in advance.

◄ This carefully posed photograph, notable for its unusually high staff/passenger ratio, shows ticket-checking at the barrier at Leicester London Road station in the 1930s.

▲ Giving information was one of the many duties of the booking office clerks, so they had to know about all the special offers and excursions that were constantly dreamed up by the marketing people and then promoted with leaflet displays in the ticket office. This example, with the entertaining graphics of its era, offers cheap day tickets in October 1961.

▶ In Victorian times the platform was a controlled area and people needed tickets even if they were not travelling. The platform ticket, varied in style and often bought from the once-familiar red penny-in-the-slot machine, remained a necessity for platform visitors through the 20th century.

SHOPS AND KIOSKS

The first station bookstall was probably opened at Fenchurch Street in London in 1841, and certainly by 1848 W H Smith had launched the chain of station newsstands and bookstalls that was to become the foundation of that empire. John Menzies started in Perth and Stirling in 1857 and before too long Smith's and Menzies controlled the station newsstand and bookstall business. Apart from the steady spread, from the end of the 19th century, of vending machines offering chocolates and confectionery, cigarettes, personal weighing and a means of printing words on a metal strip, there were no significant developments in station trading until the first fruit, sweets and snacks outlets, tobacconists, florists, bootblacks and hairdressers began to appear on the platform or the concourse. These were followed by chemists and post offices, although the postbox and the telegraph office had long been part of the station infrastructure. Station cinemas showing newsreels and cartoons were opened during the 1930s at Victoria and Waterloo in London and in Leeds, and these continued to operate at least until the 1950s, offering entertainment to those waiting for trains and somewhere warm for those wanting a place to sleep. However, unlike their American counterparts, British railway companies were slow to appreciate the potential that lay in station trading, and it was not until the 1980s that British Rail began to develop fully the station concourse shopping centre. From that point, things moved very quickly, helped inevitably by the process of privatization, and nowadays the concourses of major stations are filled with retail outlets of every kind, including many famous high street brand names selling clothing and accessories, cosmetics, stationery and food. Rental income for Network Rail and others runs in millions.

▲ The preserved railway does its best to create a period atmosphere. This is the old-style W H Smith built from scratch on Kidderminster station, on the Severn Valley Railway, photographed in 1995.

▲ Florists first appeared on stations in the 1890s, and have been there ever since. This example was photographed at Clacton-on-Sea, Essex, in 1990.

◀ This 1920s postcard shows the typically cluttered John Menzies stand on Gourock station. Menzies enjoyed a monopoly for station newsstands and bookstalls in Scotland. Adjacent to the left is the tobacconist's kiosk. The news placards declaring 'Level Crossing Smash' and 'New French Cabinet' show that nothing much changes.

▲ It is nearly 10.30 on a June morning in 1935 and the Cornish Riviera Express is about to depart from platform 1 at Paddington. Most people in this busy photograph are not catching the train but are walking along the platform or looking at the shops. There is a post office, a branch of Boots the Chemist, a tobacconist and, farther on, a confectioner, a bookstall and a hairdressing salon. Signs advertising these retail outlets are much the same as those advertising railway services.

◀ This postcard showing the small bookstall and newsstand at Bradford Midland station was posted in 1909 and indicates the relative scarcity of station retail outlets at that time. It was sent to a postcard collector in Jerusalem, with the message: 'I shall be very happy to exchange view cards with you.'

STATION GARDENS

THE IDEA OF STATION gardening probably started in the north-east of England but it quickly spread round the country, combining as it did two key principles, fostering pride in the workplace and giving satisfaction to passengers. Many stationmasters were in any case keen gardeners. Soon, a competitive element was introduced and prizes were offered for best-kept station and best station in various categories, initially on a local basis but ultimately regionally and nationally. In 1930 the LNER even fitted a bench to the front of a locomotive to speed up the judging process. Every style of gardening was featured, reflecting the tastes and skills of the station staff, but colourful schemes predominated. Today some of the best gardens are to be found on the preserved lines, but stations on the national network have not given up. Hanging baskets are commonplace and competitions still take place, often encouraged by sponsorship and local tourist boards.

▲ Raised beds on the platform, often simply made from waste materials and planted with colourful annuals, were always popular, especially if combined with the station name in flowers or painted stones. These were captured at Dulverton, in Devon, in August 1959.

ANGLO IRISH
BEST STATION COMPETITION
1992
COMMUNITY INVOLVEMENT WINNER
NORTH LLANWRST
SPONSORED BY
THE WALES TOURIST BOARD

◄ In 1992 North Llanwrst, a little station on the Conwy Valley line, won a best station award in a competition sponsored by the Wales Tourist Board. Such competitions today are often seen as community schemes.

▼ The stationmaster of Dorking North, in Surrey, proudly poses with a member of his staff in the 1930s in front of their splendid display of standard roses. Even on commuter stations, time was made for gardening, particularly in areas where the suburban garden flourished.

▲ In the mid-1990s summer colours fill the exuberant beds at Dolau, a halt on the Heart of Wales line. Railways like this, always understaffed and hovering on the edge of survival, rely on local community support.

▼ A famous miniature garden on a famous miniature railway: the rock gardens at New Romney, on the Romney, Hythe & Dymchurch in the 1930s, complete with windmill, water features and gnomes.

55. ORNAMENTAL ROCK GARDENS, WORLD'S SMALLEST RAILWAY, NEW ROMNEY STATION.

▲ Pipe in hand and surrounded by verdant plants, a GWR Inspector poses in front of his rustic pergola, probably in the garden of his house rather than on the station.

FOOD AND DRINK

Refreshment rooms are almost as old as the railways themselves. In the early days, before dining cars became commonplace, long-distance trains had scheduled meal stops at major stations such as Swindon, Carlisle and York. These were often as short as ten minutes, so there must have been mayhem at the bars and counters as passengers fought to be served. The food and drink was expensive and not very good – Charles Dickens complained that the soup and the tea tasted the same and the sandwiches were filled with sawdust. Things did improve, however, and by the end of the Victorian era some station restaurants were richly decorated, highly regarded and widely used by the general public as well as railway travellers. Most railway catering was leased to contractors, a pattern maintained until nationalization, when British Railways had its own hotel and restaurant division. This coincided with a move to self-service cafeterias, eventually brought together in 1973 under the Travellers Fare name. After privatization, station catering was thrown wide open to fast food outlets, famous chains, specialist bars and buffets, and other independent operators. Old-style refreshment rooms have also returned to some smaller stations.

▲ There have been many attempts to improve the quality of refreshments, particularly for those prepared to pay premium prices. Typical is the Pullman Lounge, making the most of a famous name.

▼ Station catering today is informal. One of many names operating on the platform is Pumpkin, seen here at Taunton, in the old GWR refreshment room.

LAKE SIDE REFRESHMENT PAVILION.   LAKE SIDE STATION (WINDERMERE).

▲ Many refreshment rooms were equipped with branded crockery, now collector's items. This Minton cup features the elaborate monogram that was used briefly by the LNER during the 1920s.

▼ Wemyss Bay was a station noted for its setting, its floral displays, its circular booking hall and, not least, its very homely tearoom, featured here on an Edwardian postcard issued by the Caledonian Railway.

▲ The refreshment pavilion at Lakeside station was justly famous for its setting and views over Windermere and was widely used by the public as well as rail travellers. This promotional postcard was issued by the Furness Railway in the Edwardian era.

▲ Refreshment rooms at stations were regularly updated, to reflect contemporary styles. This carefully posed promotional picture shows a recently refurbished room at an unnamed station, redolent with smart Art Deco detailing.

WAITING

Early railway companies often treated their passengers without much care or attention, and few stations offered any degree of comfort. If waiting rooms were provided they were generally gloomy and ill-equipped places. Indeed, the novelist Anthony Trollope described the facilities at Taunton as 'hideous, dirty and disagreeable'. By the middle of the 19th century things were much better, and large stations often had a sequence of waiting rooms, catering for first, second and third class passengers, and separate areas for women. Smaller stations offered three rooms, first class, ladies, and general, and even on the smallest stations there was usually a separate room for ladies, something that has survived in a few places to the present day. There were also lavatories for ladies and gentlemen from an early date, sometimes combined with waiting rooms, and these were among the first public lavatories in Britain. Standards varied considerably. At the worst, the waiting room was an open-fronted wooden shed with a hard bench, at the best there were upholstered seats, pictures and posters on the walls and, in winter, a roaring fire, features that made waiting for a train a relaxed and pleasant experience. Some stations had private waiting rooms, notably those used by the royal family and certain members of the aristocracy and their visitors. At Wolferton, the station for Sandringham, there were three royal waiting rooms. In recent years the waiting room has started to disappear, particularly at major stations, where it has been replaced by open seating on the concourse. By the same token, it was British Rail that started the logical process of merging the waiting room and the buffet.

▶ In about 1910 an amateur photographer took this evocative view of passengers waiting at London's Holborn Viaduct station. A sailor sleeps on his kitbag and two men are in desultory conversation on benches that are surprisingly near to the platform edge. Even the South Eastern & Chatham locomotives seem to be waiting for something to happen.

▲ Shepton Mallet Charlton Road station was on the Somerset & Dorset line. The gentlemen's lavatory looks pretty basic and seems to have faced out on to the platform. However, when travellers depended on station lavatories this was better than nothing.

▼ Farrington Gurney was a halt on the GWR line from Radstock to Bristol via Pensford. It had one platform and the most basic of waiting rooms. There was a separate ticket office, in a little room behind the Miner's Arms public house. On this grey day in the 1930s a single, smartly dressed passenger waits, preferring the platform to the wooden shelter.

▲ Waiting rooms today are relative rarities so passengers tend to wait on the platforms, taking advantage of the new generation of steel station benches. This is Malton in 2005, where most of the buildings are closed or given over to other purposes. Quite a crowd is waiting for the train to York.

WAITING · AND LADIES ROOMS

▲ Maidenhead acquired a new waiting room in 1943, a fully glazed structure in the centre of the platform. The clearly visible interior made it safe for women, who on this station had to share the room with male travellers. At that time this was an unusual situation on larger stations.

SOMETHING DIFFERENT

DOCKS AND HARBOURS

The great expansion of docks and harbours in Victorian Britain was driven directly by the spreading railway network, and from the 1840s railway companies were actively involved in dock development. New docks were planned from the start to be served by the railway, with notable examples in Hull and London in the 1850s. At about the same time, railway companies began to appreciate the advantages of owning the docks they served, thereby having control over development, management and pricing. As a result, railways were the driving force behind the creation of many new dock complexes, with famous examples being Barrow, built from nothing by the Furness Railway, the Great Western's new docks at Millbay in Plymouth and Fishguard, and Goole, a development by the Lancashire & Yorkshire company. This pattern continued through the latter part of the Victorian era and into the 20th century. The greatest railway port was Southampton, bought by the LSWR in 1892 and massively developed by that company and its successor, the Southern Railway, to the point where it overtook Liverpool in both passenger and freight business. After the Grouping of 1923 the

▼ Kyle of Lochalsh, formerly the ferry point for the Isle of Skye, owed its development to the Highland Railway, whose long branch from Inverness finally arrived in 1897. For years it was busy with Skye traffic, and here, in 1965, there is still plenty of freight, but today the road bridge takes it all.

▶ Glasson dock was created by the Lancaster Canal and contributed hugely to that company's success. In 1883 a branch line was built from Lancaster to serve the dock, adding to its success. This 1890s photograph shows Glasson Dock station still looking spic and span. The line closed in 1964.

▲ The Falmouth branch is one of few in Cornwall to survive, kept open during the closures of the 1960s by the then still busy Falmouth harbour. Since then things have changed and Falmouth Docks station is little more than a name, a single track and its distinctive building, seen here in 1990.

GWR found itself the largest dock-owning company in the world.

Most railway docks were for general traffic, but some handled specific products, such as coal or fish. Other harbours were linked to passenger-carrying services, notably across the Irish Sea, the English Channel and the North Sea. This started in 1844, with the purchase of Folkestone harbour by the South Eastern Railway, and then spread around the coast of Britain as rival companies competed for passenger and freight traffic. Cross-channel ports in southern England included Weymouth, Portsmouth, Southampton, Newhaven, Folkestone, Dover, Ramsgate, Queenborough and Port Victoria on the Isle of Grain. Irish routes were equally competitive; ports included Fishguard, Holyhead, Liverpool, Heysham, Stranraer, Ardrossan and Glasgow. Another development was the train ferry, the first of which operated across the Forth from 1849. However, significant development of train ferry traffic did not occur until World War I, with the special ports at Harwich, Southampton, Dover and Richborough in Kent. A few train ferry services survived until the opening of the Channel Tunnel. Alongside major dock developments, such as Grangemouth in Scotland and Grimsby and Immingham around the Humber, there were also hundreds of small ports and harbours scattered along the coastline. Many had existed for centuries but were given a new lease of life by railway connections. Wherever possible, lines were laid along ancient quays – typical examples include Pembroke, Kyle of Lochalsh, Falmouth, Rye, Brightlingsea, Looe and Whitby. In other places entirely new harbours were created by railways.

▲ This delightfully posed postcard view shows Heysham station in the Edwardian era. One of the many harbour stations built for the Irish trade and reached via Lancaster, it was never as busy as some of its rivals. In the platform is a motor train, an early example of a push-pull multiple unit.

▲ The ambitious Manchester, Sheffield & Lincolnshire Railway reached Hull via a ferry service across the Humber. Started in the 1840s, this continued to operate until 1981, when the Humber bridge was opened. The result of this was a station that had no railway and whose passengers came and went by boat. Known as Corporation Pier station, and shown here in the 1970s, it was, and still is, a handsome building.

▼ Passengers travelling to and from Hull by the ferry used the railway to New Holland Pier, where the tracks stopped literally at the river's edge. Never the most convenient route to Hull, it was nonetheless busy in the 19th century. By the time this photograph was taken, in 1981, the station was clearly on its last legs.

▲ Built by the Pembroke & Tenby Railway with the backing of the GWR, Pembroke Dock station was a typical small-scale GWR terminus. It opened in 1864, and in 1871 the line was extended to serve the Admiralty docks. When photographed in 1972, it retained many original features, some of which survive.

WHY DID WE GO THERE?

SCARBOROUGH joined the railway network in 1845 and from that date this old town flourished as a resort. Visitors could enjoy its harbour, beach, spa and castle and, thanks to the arrival of connecting lines, they could also explore the Yorkshire coast, the moors and dales, and the nearby towns and cities. Whitby, York and Harrogate were all within striking distance by train, making Scarborough a popular destination for rail excursions.

NORTH EASTERN RAILWAY.

From

SCARBOROUGH

THE SUN
...ST COAST

No. R 906

HALF-DAY
EXCURSION

...CARBORO'
WHIT-MONDAY

OUTWARD JOURNEY		3rd Return	RETURN JOURNEY	
LEEDS (City) ... dep 11 0	am	s d 4 9	SCARBOROUGH dep 11 20	pm
SCARBOROUGH arr 12 40 (Londesborough Rd Station)	pm		LEEDS (City) ... arr 1 10	am

...s and trams for all main routes will depart from City Square after the arrival of return train at Leeds (Fare 4d).

TICKETS CAN BE OBTAINED IN ADVANCE

'RIPS from SCARBOROUGH (Lighthouse Pier) on the motor ships "Coronia" w Royal Lady" are available at the reduced charge of 1/8 (Afternoon Trips—2 hours— ...m) and 10d (Evening Trips—1 hour—at 6.30 pm) on presentation of return halves of excursion tickets.

...s and all particulars can be obtained at Leeds (City) Headingley Horsforth and ... Stations, or from the usual Agencies.

YOUR HOLIDAY HANDBOOK 6d
...m L·N·E·R Stations Offices & Agencies

...rmation apply to the District Passenger Manager, Leeds, Tel 20615.
Monthly Return Tickets are available by these trains.

CONDITIONS OF ISSUE
...ing Tickets are issued subject to the conditions applicable to tickets of these descriptions as shown ...e Tables.
...years of age, Free ; three years and under fourteen, Half-fares.
For LUGGAGE ALLOWANCES also see Time Tables.

3742—Petty & Sons Ltd Leeds—5,000

SCARBOROUGH.—THE SPA PROMENADE.

▲ Scarborough was a popular rail excursion destination and remained so into the 1960s, when many of the connecting lines were closed down.

▲ The message on this 1903 card says it all: 'Mr Johnson and myself are spending a weekend here. It really is very smart. The journey via Coast Route was very beautiful. The weather fine & the folk quite giddy.'

▶ Scarborough was the gateway to the delights of the moors and dales of North Yorkshire.

Bogs Valley Gardens, Harrogate

◄ The journey from Scarborough to the famous old spa town of Harrogate was quite simple, involving one change in York. Arthur Newton, holidaying there in April 1904, sent this card to all his friends in Manchester, via Miss Doman: 'Kind regards to all you know I know.'

◄ Visitors to Scarborough could easily enjoy a day out seeing the sights of York and shopping in its medieval streets. This Edwardian card shows the famous Shambles.

Shambles York.

VIEW ACROSS RIVER WHITBY FROM MARKET HOUSE

W. Manthurn

▲ The train journey along the coast from Scarborough to Whitby was one of the best in Britain. Many visitors took it as much for the views as for the pleasure of exploring Whitby's old harbour and ancient streets.

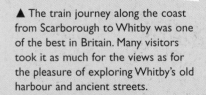

49086. BRIDLINGTON. FLORAL CLOCK, ROYAL PRINCES PARADE.

◄ In 1906, when this card was sent, Bridlington was a smart resort a short train journey to the south of Scarborough. Gardens and floral displays, and particularly floral clocks, were a feature of the coastal resorts of north-east England.

AIRPORT AND INTERNATIONAL

In the Victorian era, thanks to competition between rival railway companies, there were many more stations offering international services than now. Trains met ships at harbour and dock stations all around the coast of Britain, with scheduled services to connect with ferries to many European and Irish ports. Equally important were the city termini from which international, or rather boat, trains departed. In London these included Paddington, Euston, Liverpool Street, Victoria, Waterloo, Charing Cross and Blackfriars. Today, in the age of genuinely international trains via the Channel Tunnel, the number of departure stations is much reduced.

While the relationship between railways and ferries has generally been clear-cut, that between railways and airlines has been more complex. In 1929 the railways were given powers by Parliament to operate air services, and the 1930s saw the Southern, the Great Western and the LMS doing so. Typical routes were Croydon to the Isle of Wight, Plymouth to Liverpool, and London to Belfast and Glasgow. The start of World War II brought it all to an end but by 1944, it seems, the railway companies had ambitions to operate air services all over Europe. This came to nothing. The next phase was the more practical one of opening stations to serve airports. Gatwick and Birmingham International were among the first; others have followed, including Manchester, Southampton, Stanstead, Heathrow, Cardiff and London City.

▲ At first the Great Eastern operated its international services from Harwich Town, but lack of space resulted in a move to a brand new site 2 miles further inland. Parkeston Quay opened in 1882 and quickly became a major centre for international traffic, helped by a large new hotel. The station and its facilities have changed considerably since this photograph was taken in the early 1900s.

▶ Today, Blackfriars is a small Thameslink commuter station in London but when it was opened in the 1860s by the South Eastern Railway it had far grander ambitions. Little survives from the original station, but notable are the stone panels carved with the names of destinations. There are wonderful juxtapositions: Baden Baden and Beckenham, Berlin and Bickley.

▲ Originally a station on the coastal route from Cardiff Bridgend, Rhoose was closed in the 1960s. In 2005 the line was reopened and the new Rhoose became the station for Cardiff airport.

◀ Seen here in 1994, Birmingham International was conceived from the start as a dual purpose station, serving the airport and the National Exhibition Centre. It was built on a greenfield site in characteristic late 20th-century style. It is a classic of its time.

PITCH AND TURF

The ability of the railways to move large numbers of people quickly and cheaply had a direct impact upon sport across the country. Most affected was horse-racing. By the 1840s lines had reached a number of racecourses, including Newmarket and Chester, enabling both spectators and horses to be transported there. Later, some special racecourse stations were built, such as Newbury. The railways also changed the face of football, making fixtures possible between teams that were miles apart, and running football specials for spectators. The numbers conveyed by train were huge – over 200,000 for the 1923 cup final at Wembley between Bolton and West Ham – and football specials were important revenue earners for railway companies for over a century. Grounds were often sited close to railway lines. Other spectator sports to benefit from special train services included rugby and cricket. The first dedicated cricket station was Old Trafford, and in 1878 special trains helped to make the first Australian tour a success.

▲ In 1958, when this handbill was produced, spectators still relied on the railways for their transport to test matches and other important cricket fixtures.

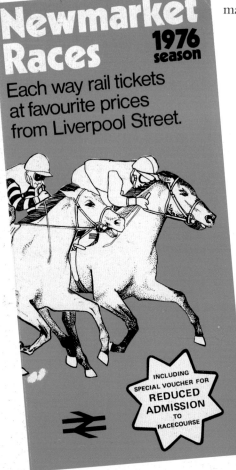

▲ The railways' continuing involvement with horse-racing is underlined by promotional leaflets such as this 1976 example.

◄ Rugby supporters crowd the platform at Newport in 1999, perhaps on their way to the Millennium Stadium – a ground whose success was assured by its proximity to a station.

▲ One of the few dedicated racecourse stations still operating is Newbury, positioned right by the course. An old GWR station sign marks the special platform used by the race-day trains from Paddington and Bristol.

▼ Between the early 1930s and 1968 West Bromwich Albion's ground was served by its own station, The Hawthorns Halt, one of the only stations to open regularly on Christmas Day. Here, on 25 March 1961, a few spectators make their way to the ground. Clearly it was not a very important match.

CLIFF, BEACH AND PIER RAILWAYS

THE BRITISH LOVE of the seaside inspired a number of unusual railway systems. The primary example was the cliff railway, the first of which was opened at Scarborough in 1875 and the most recent at Bournemouth in 1935. At the peak of development there were 21 at seaside resorts and four inland. Of these, 17 are still in operation. Operated by cable and gravity systems, usually double-tracked and steeply graded, and equipped with cars full of period detail, these represent a rare survival of Victorian enterprise in the modern world. Also popular were beach and pier railways, the latter often developed from the simple tracks laid to facilitate construction of the pier or from basic railways built to carry baggage to and from steamers arriving at the end of the pier. The first passenger-carrying pier railway opened at Ryde, on the Isle of Wight, in 1864 and many others followed, for example at Southend, Herne Bay, Southport, Hythe, Walton-on-the-Naze, Felixstowe and Blackpool. Traction was initially by horse and later by cable, electricity, petrol or diesel. The longest was at Southend, one of the last to survive, having been totally rebuilt in the 1980s. As with cliff railways, a variety of gauges were used and the cars were delightfully varied.

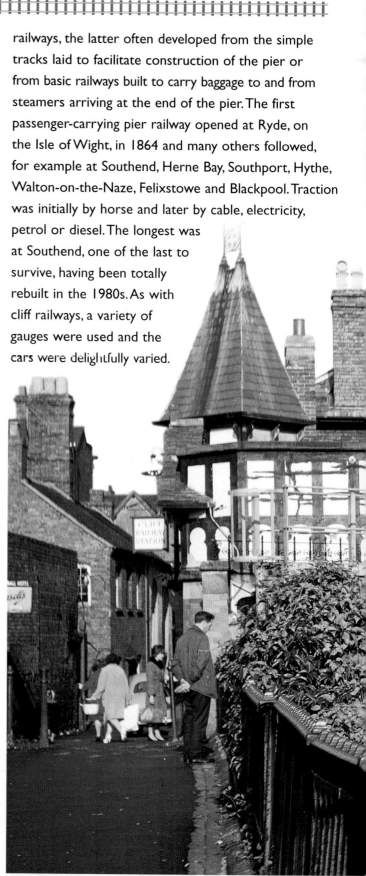

▲ The Lynton & Lynmouth Cliff Railway is, at 890ft, the longest in Britain. Journey time is about two minutes. This Edwardian card shows the style of car, the long track, the counter-balanced cable haulage – and the spirit of adventure that these railways represented.

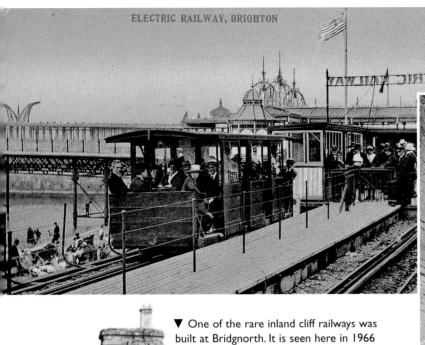
ELECTRIC RAILWAY, BRIGHTON

◀ In 1883 Magnus Volk opened the world's first electric-powered railway along the beach in Brighton, from Palace Pier to Black Rock. Still in operation, this extraordinary railway combines history with the fun of the seaside.

▼ One of the rare inland cliff railways was built at Bridgnorth. It is seen here in 1966 and, remarkably, it continues to operate today. Notable are the Art Deco-style cars, echoing the look of 1930s motor coaches.

EAST HILL LIFT HASTINGS.

▲ When it opened in 1902, the East Hill Lift in Hastings was the steepest cliff railway in Britain, necessitating the high cars shown in this Edwardian view. It still runs today. The distance is short, but the stations are substantial and impressive.

▲ This lady looks ready to enjoy her trip along the Hythe pier tramway in Hampshire in the summer of 1959. Opened in 1880 to transport baggage, this 2ft-gauge line later carried passengers. It has used electric power since 1922.

LITTLE TRAINS OF WALES

In the early 19th century narrow gauge railways were used extensively in construction projects and in industry. At that point, narrow gauge meant anything less than standard gauge but was usually between 2ft and 4ft. There were many variations: 2ft, 2ft 3in and 2ft 8in were all used in Wales. Narrow gauge lines, temporary or permanent, were cheap to build, and men or horses supplied the motive power until the 1850s, when small locomotives began to appear. By the 1870s a number of builders were specializing in narrow gauge track and equipment. Most railways were built to serve mines or quarries and to make connections with main lines or ports, but industrial use was also common. Wales became a centre for narrow gauge lines, many of which, for example the Ffestiniog and the Talyllyn, were associated with the slate industry. For much of the 19th century passenger carrying was incidental, but the growth of tourism in the last decades of Victoria's reign gave the railways a new lease of life. Existing lines started passenger services and new lines opened for the tourist market, notably the Vale of Rheidol, the Snowdon Mountain and the Welsh Highland. In the 1940s and 1950s railway preservation began with Welsh narrow gauge lines, and today at least 13 lines are in operation in Wales.

▲ The Brecon Mountain Railway is a relatively new narrow gauge line, laid along 3.5 miles of the former standard gauge Merthyr & Brecon railway. The locomotive fleet includes examples from Germany and South Africa. At Pontsticill station, the booking office was in a former goods van.

▼ The Welsh Highland Railway, now one of the most ambitious railway restoration projects in Britain, had a chequered career. The first attempt at a line from Porthmadog to Caernarfon started in 1901 but it was not until 1923 that it finally opened, only for it to close in 1936. As this photograph of Portmadoc New indicates, some facilities were pretty basic.

The Glyn Valley Train.

▲ In this Edwardian postcard, the locomotive 'Sir Theodore' waits to depart along the Glyn Valley Tramway. Driver and fireman pose in typical style but the group of children ignore the proceedings. The railway, along the Glyn valley, near Ellesmere, opened in 1874. Steam traction for passenger trains was introduced in 1891. Closure came in 1935 as a result of road competition.

◄ Little girls and old men look on and passengers lean from the windows as Talyllyn locomotive no. 2 'Dolgoch', a veteran of 1866, prepares to draw its train out of Towyn Wharf station. Built as a slate line, the Talyllyn was firmly established in the tourist business when this postcard was issued in the 1930s.

Snowdon Mountain Railway,

Snowdon. Summit and Train.

▶ When this card was sent in 1903, the Snowdon Mountain Railway had been in operation for only six years. Travelling to the summit along the 5 miles of the steep rack line was still a novelty, as was the special summit postmark used here. The note says: 'Summit Aug 11th 3.15. Climbed in 2 hrs. Grand view.' Most people take the train up and walk down – perhaps the sender did it the other way round.

PRESERVED STATIONS

The idea that closed railways could be brought back to life and run by volunteers emerged in the late 1940s, with the initial focus on Welsh narrow gauge lines. In the 1960s the emphasis switched to standard gauge and, inspired by the closures that followed the recommendations of the Beeching report, a major preservation movement erupted in all parts of Britain. At the same time, the phasing out of steam haulage by British Railways greatly speeded up locomotive preservation. The result was a spreading network of privately owned sections of line, along which steam trains could be operated for the pleasure of visitors. Today there are over 100 preserved lines and steam centres in Britain and hundreds of steam and diesel locomotives have been brought back from the dead, enabling millions of people to enjoy an historic experience on a regular basis. All preserved lines need stations and many have been restored for regular use, usually in the style of a perceived golden age of railways. Where the stations did not exist, they have been brought from other places or built from scratch, but with the same meticulous concern for detail as the preserved examples. A station, fully equipped in period style, is therefore the start and finish of the preserved railway experience, presented in such a way a to appeal both to those old enough to have known the real thing, and to younger people happy to enjoy a romantic dream. There are now preserved railways all over the world, but Britain is the centre of the steam movement.

▼ In the 1990s the Embsay & Bolton Abbey Steam Railway extended its line in Yorkshire and built from scratch a new station at Bolton Abbey, following precisely the Midland Railway style of the 1890s. Detailed replicas of this kind add to the atmosphere of the steam railway experience.

▲ The concern for period detail is evident in the restored booking office at Shackerstone, headquarters of the Battlefield Steam Railway in Leicestershire. It reopened on 9 July 1989.

◄ The North Yorkshire Moors Railway was early on the preservation scene and its 18-mile route is one of the longest. At Grosmont in the 1970s a visiting special from British Rail has brought out the crowds.

▼ A preserved steam line that has made itself indistinguishable from the original is the Isle of Wight Steam Railway. The old buildings at Haven Street survived, so it was relatively simple to turn the clock back to the the British Railways era of the 1950s.

BITS AND PIECES

The PLEASURES of railways are manifold. For most people, the emphasis has always been on the trains themselves, which have woven their way deeply into the British psyche. Far more significant, however, have been the buildings and structures, and the permanent impact these have made upon landscape and history. Yet even more appealing, both to the enthusiast and the casually curious, is the vast amount of paraphernalia with which the railways surrounded themselves. These are, literally, the bits and pieces of history, small things that can still tell big stories. Some were universal, essential things that made the railways operate smoothly; others were quirky and idiosyncratic. Many carried the stamp of particular railway companies, and there were delightful and infinite local variations. There was plenty to be seen long after the formation of the national rail network. Survivors, rarer now, pass regularly through specialist railwayana sales and fairs, but for the observant and sometimes eagle-eyed traveller there is still much to enjoy.

▲ The station lamp came in many forms and styles. A number of companies incorporated the station name into the lamp to help passengers at night. Chathill was a NER station in Northumberland.

▲ In the early 1960s plenty survived from the days of the independent railway companies despite British Railways' desire for a uniform style. Much was eccentric and decidedly local, including this untypical GWR train indicator fingerpost at Talyllyn Junction, a once busy place near the Welsh borders, seen here in 1962.

THIS RAILWAY STATION WAS USED AS A
TEA STALL FOR SAILORS AND SOLDIERS FROM
20TH SEPTEMBER 1915, UNTIL 12TH APRIL 1919
IN CONNECTION WITH THE ROSS AND CROMARTY
COUNTY BRANCH RED CROSS SOCIETY.
DURING WHICH PERIOD 134,864 MEN WERE
SUPPLIED WITH TEA.

I & A.J. RWY.   I & A.J. RWY.

THIS RAILWAY EXTENDING FROM THE TOWN OF NAIRN TO KEITH,
COMPLETING THE COMMUNICATION BETWEEN LONDON AND INVERNESS,
WAS BEGUN IN OCT 1856 AND OPENED FOR PUBLIC TRAFFIC ON 18 AUGUST 1858:
AND THIS VIADUCT CROSSING THE SPEY WAS COMPLETED IN 20 MONTHS.
CONTRACTORS FOR MASONRY, DAVID MITCHELL AND CHAS. BRAND. MONTROSE.
FOR IRON WORK. MESSRS. FAIRBAIRN AND SONS. MANCHESTER.
ENGINEER JOSEPH MITCHELL F.R.S.E. INVERNESS.

▲ Dingwall station is a remote spot in the Highlands of Scotland, yet it has played its part in history as a stopping point on the way to military and naval bases. This well-polished plaque still proudly announces that between September 1915 and April 1919 the ladies of the local Red Cross served 134,864 cups of tea.

▲ Many stations still carry ceremonial panels or name plaques. A reflection of the pride that railway builders took in their achievements, they can also reveal the intricacies of railway history. This famous cast-iron example at Inverness station was erected by the Inverness & Aberdeen Junction Railway in 1858.

▲ Certain objects reveal intimate details of railway life. Until well into the 20th century many remote signal boxes and crossing-keepers' cottages had neither running water nor electricity. Water supplies were delivered daily by passing trains in containers such as these, ready and waiting at Edington Birtle, in Somerset, in 1965. The handle seen on the right of the picture lowers an oil lamp for cleaning, filling and wick-trimming.

◄ Thousands of local sidings all over the country required thousands of ground frames to operate the points. Despite modern technology, there are plenty of survivors to be seen, some of which are in use. This ancient pair of points levers, complete with lock, was still operational in the 1990s at Battersby, formerly a busy junction on the Whitby line.

► The railways and the mail grew up together, so many stations were equipped with postboxes, frequently set into the wall. When railways or stations closed, the mailbox often remained, with its enamel name plaque. This VR box was photographed long after the Hawkhurst branch, in Kent, had gone, still displaying its battered Horsmonden Station plaque.

MINIATURE RAILWAYS

The distinction between narrow gauge and miniature railways is not clear, but the latter tend to be built to a gauge that is 18in or less. Miniature railways were first promoted in the late Victorian period by Sir Arthur Heywood, who built a 15in-gauge line on his estate near Derby to demonstrate the practical passenger- and freight-carrying possibilities of the miniature railway. His vision of a national network of miniature lines linking estates, villages and remote regions to the main lines was not to be realized, but by the Edwardian era the potential for tourism offered by such lines was being appreciated. However, the real heyday of the miniature railway was the 1920s and 1930s, with a notable example being the 15in-gauge Romney, Hythe & Dymchurch Railway in Kent. During this period many miniature railways were built, both as practical passenger-carrying lines and as tourist attractions. Indeed, there came a time when few seaside resorts and parks did not boast a miniature railway of some kind or another. Some used locomotives that were scaled-down versions of the real thing, while others adapted industrial vehicles. More common today, particularly among enthusiasts, are lines built to a smaller gauge, 7in or less, with passengers sitting astride the vehicles.

▲ Kerr's Miniature Railway opened as a tourist line in Arbroath, Angus, in 1935 and by 1937 was carrying over 20,000 passengers per year. By the 1950s this had risen to 60,000, but a decline then followed and the line faced closure in the late 1970s. Since then it has been extensively restored and rebuilt.

▶ Built in 1895 as a 15in-gauge line linking Fairbourne village with Penrhyn Point, Gwynedd, the Fairbourne & Barmouth Railway has had a chequered career but is now enjoying success once more. Rebuilt to a smaller gauge in 1984, the line is famous for its setting and for its locomotives, which are half-size replicas of classic narrow gauge engines.

◀ A typical seaside resort railway was built in Southport, Lancashire, by George Llewellyn from 1911. With its scaled-down replica locomotives and tall passenger vehicles, this was a proper miniature railway, as indicated by this Edwardian postcard.

◀ A typical enthusiasts' and model makers' miniature railway is the Heath Park line near Cardiff, photographed here in 1991. The locomotives used on such a line are normally meticulously made scale models, such as the GWR 'Manor' shown here. Such lines, often run by clubs, are usually for demonstration purposes, and passengers make short journeys sitting astride the vehicles.

▶ A number of miniature railways were built to serve private estates, the first being that opened at the Duke of Westminster's Eaton Hall, in Cheshire, in 1898. These had both practical and entertainment functions. This Edwardian postcard shows the Blakesley Hall line, a working miniature railway built by C W Bartholomew from 1903 to serve his Towcester estate, in Northamptonshire.

MINIATURE RAILWAY, BLAKESLEY HALL

WISH YOU WERE HERE!
NORTHERN ENGLAND

*I*N NORTHERN ENGLAND *railway station postcards are as diverse as ever. There are plenty of views of the major stations, with York being the most common, but photographers seem to have been drawn particularly to the remoter corners of the network. Before World War I the railway station was for many still a novelty and, at the same time, it was the centre of social and commercial life. It is notable that in many cases the photographer has picked a quiet moment, with plenty of time to set the scene and pose the people in front of the camera. These pictures are not about trains. In any case, slow exposures made it hard to photograph trains.*

▶ *York is a common postcard subject and this is the favourite viewpoint, showing the great curve of the iron and glass trainshed roof, the crowning glory of the 1870s station. For a busy station, the photographer has chosen a remarkably quiet moment, with no trains and very few people in view.*

KIRBYMOORSIDE.

◀ *For an Edwardian postcard, this is an unusually busy view, photographed from the footbridge at Kirkbymoorside station, east of York. A train is drawing into the platform while people stand and wait in conveniently satisfactory but unposed groups, mostly unaware of the camera. There are parcels and luggage to be loaded, and everyone is well dressed.*

Arnside Station.

L'byland Series 11847.

◄ It is a quiet day at Arnside, in about 1905 and two porters have plenty of time to pose. The oddly composed view, with the lamp in the centre, shows the timber-framed building and the elaborate iron benches favoured by the Furness Railway. At this time Arnside, on the Cumbrian coast, was a junction station.

► The Dandy One Horse Railway is the title of this delightful 1912 card. It shows the famous passenger service to Port Carlisle on Silloth Bay, opened in 1856 and horse-drawn until 1914. Passenger services ceased entirely in 1932. Masterfully posed, the photograph captures the flavour of this unique railway. One Dandy car survives, in the National Railway Museum in York.

Dandy One Horse Railway, Port Carlisle.

◄ Wylam is famous in railway history as the birthplace of George Stephenson. The station, west of Newcastle, was a busy place, but not in 1913, when this photograph was taken. The crossing gates are shut and the few passengers stand still for the camera. The writer, Miss Ormston, said: 'Will be at Alston with the 12.15. Be sure and turn up to meet your dearly beloved.' Let's hope he did.

TOY STATIONS

HORNBY-DUBLO

STATION NAMES

To be affixed to station nameboards with Seccotine or cellulose adhesive

MECCANO LTD · ENGLAND

LICHFIELD   LICHFIELD

OVERTON   OVERTON

WESTBURY   WESTBURY

NEWARK   NEWARK

CRAWFORD   CRAWFORD

Like the railways themselves, toy trains were a creation of the Victorian era. Initially Germany, traditionally the centre for the making of toys and automata, dominated the market. The first generation of metal toy trains were large, not particularly accurate in scale or detail, and were played with on the carpet. Rails came later, along with a greater concern for detail. By the end of the 19th century train sets were readily available, made in Germany for the British market by manufacturers such as Bing and Marklin and replicating the styles and colours of British railway companies. With them came the first ranges of accessories, stations, engine sheds, signals, lighting and so on. However, they were still big – gauge 0, 1 or even larger. During World War I there was a reaction against all things German and this gave British companies an opening. Bassett-Lowke and later Hornby took the market by storm with their model railways, complete in every detail. Initially 0 gauge dominated, but then in the 1930s Hornby introduced 00-gauge, marketed as the tabletop railway. This really opened up the market and toy railways achieved a remarkable popularity. This was also the point of divide between the toy and the model, with serious railway modellers preferring the precision of the smaller 00-gauge, with its almost infinite ranges of accessories. Complex model railways for public display were built all over Britain, clubs were established, and many manufacturers joined the game, offering ever more adventurous models and construction kits. At the heart of every layout there was a station.

British Railways Model Railway

▲ From the 1920s to the 1960s Hornby offered a wonderful range of 0-gauge toy railways and accessories that made the most of the printed tin technology for which their Liverpool factory was so famous. This display suggests a terminus station at the end of a GWR branch line in Wales or the West Country, in the 1940s or 1950s.

▲ Ivo Peters, the famous railway enthusiast and photographer, had his own 0-gauge layout, which he photographed with the same precision as the real thing. To the left is a pack of 00-gauge station names, issued by Hornby in the 1950s.

◄ In 1948 British Railways created a huge model railway, covering over 700sq ft, to demonstrate to young and old the intricacies of modern railway operations. Much of the layout and some of the models that ran on it were made by British Railways' staff in their own workshops. It was complete with stations, railway structures, houses, farms, trees and animals. The layout was designed to travel the country and it was seen in various locations in the 1950s by some 250,000 people a year.

▲ From the 1930s many manufacturers issued catalogues of model railways and accessories, showing both factory-made products and construction kits. Above is a pack of plans for stations and other railway buildings issued by the Hobbies Company of Norfolk in the 1950s and (top) an image from a Hornby catalogue of 1979 showing 00-gauge station buildings.

◄ Model railways built for public display were opened all over Britain from the 1930s. A typical example is the Timrow railway, commemorated by this souvenir postcard.

PUBLICITY AND PROMOTION

RAILWAY PUBLICITY

In the Victorian period railway publicity tended to be direct and to the point, concentrating on routes, fares, timetables, excursions and so on, usually presented in bold typography. Ceramics and enamel were used for more durable notices. Colour-printed posters first appeared in the 1870s but it was not until the Edwardian era that these began to achieve a distinctive style and quality, coincidental with a more sophisticated view of advertising and publicity. Before World War I leading companies began to concern themselves about image and house style, and this trend became more apparent after the formation of

▲ The British Rail image of the 1960s and 1970s maintained the traditions of the 1950s in the use of typography and illustrations but achieved a more modern look.

▲ In the 1950s clean typography, classic sans serif lettering and humorous illustrations were often combined to make even simple leaflets appealing.

◄ Totally in the spirit of its age is this entertaining 1977 Motorail brochure, complete with butterfly and fantasy landscape, with a design approach reminiscent of the record covers of that time.

▲ Some companies had route maps made in ceramic tiles for use at stations. A few survive, in effect living history. Historic too is the adjacent poster, a record of British Rail's long-gone holiday business.

the Big Four, all of which companies were highly design conscious. Posters were commissioned from leading artists, and great efforts were made to make stations tidier and more user friendly, and to ensure information was readily accessible. This approach was maintained by British Railways through the various changes of house style widely applied to publicity material in the 1950s, 1960s and 70s, and the 1980s. Illustrations and photographs were often combined with enterprising design to make memorable images.

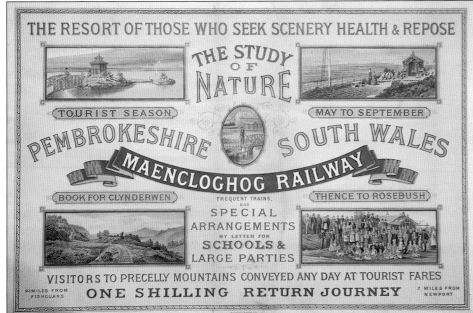

▲ In the early 1960s British Railways produced a rather spicy set of travel posters promoting various holiday regions. The design was interesting and of its period, bringing together typography, illustration, collage – and, here, a sultry bathing beauty. At this point, the 1940s totem symbol was still in use, but it was on the way out.

◀ Photographed in 1963, this enamel sign proved to be more durable than the railway it was made to promote. The Maencloghog was an obscure and short-lived line, incorporated into the North Pembroke & Fishguard Railway. It was opened in 1898, operated by the GWR and, after a chequered career, closed in 1937. In World War II the line was used for target practice by the RAF and the USAF, and Maencloghog tunnel was used for training with Barnes Wallis's bouncing bombs.

ADVERTISING

Railways were quick to realize the value of stations as vehicles for advertising and therefore as sources of income, thanks to the ever-increasing number of people using the network through the 19th century. Initially, stations displayed information about train services but this was quickly expanded into other areas in response to the Victorian love of promotion and publicity. Early advertisements were usually monochrome and relied for their impact upon a variety of letterforms printed as large as possible. However, dramatic advances in technology changed all this in the second half of the 19th century and colour printing, first used widely in the form of chromolithography from the 1840s, made possible the production of full-colour posters. These began to appear in the 1880s, promoting both railway services and consumer products and by the early 1900s the poster was well established not only as an efficient selling tool but also an increasingly adventurous artistic medium. At the same time, the large-scale production of enamel signs began to change radically the appearance of the station. Signs in bright enamel colours durably fired on to large sheets of tin were the ideal advertising medium. Eye-catching, long-lasting, weatherproof and damage resistant, they spread quickly

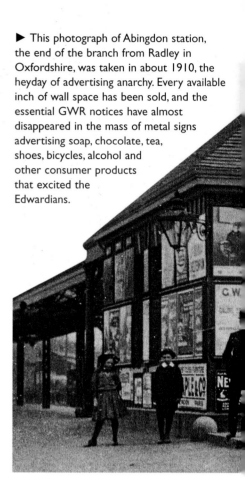

▶ This photograph of Abingdon station, the end of the branch from Radley in Oxfordshire, was taken in about 1910, the heyday of advertising anarchy. Every available inch of wall space has been sold, and the essential GWR notices have almost disappeared in the mass of metal signs advertising soap, chocolate, tea, shoes, bicycles, alcohol and other consumer products that excited the Edwardians.

▲ Colourful enamel signs were a decorative revenue earner on stations all over Britain from the late Victorian period to the 1950s, and smoking requisites were always well represented. Now collectable in their own right, enamel signs are a familiar period feature on preserved lines. This rose-bordered but battered Swan Vestas sign is at Staverton Bridge on the South Devon Railway.

▼ No. 5624 arrives at Pontllanfraith (Low Level), an old GWR station in south Wales, with a Neath train on 27 July 1963. The waiting passengers cannot have failed to notice that the local brewery is making the most of the advertising space offered by the footbridge.

along platform fences and soon made their way on to the actual buildings, both inside and out. Railway companies were quick to sell every possible inch of space, not just on station buildings, but also on bridges and other lineside structures. In the absence of any planning constraints it was a free-for-all, and in many cases the actual station notices became hard to distinguish. Order was imposed on this chaos in the 1930s by image-conscious railways, but station advertising has remained a vital revenue earner. Enamel signs live on, but only in the curious timewarp inhabited by preserved lines.

ON THE SCREEN

TRAINS FEATURE in some of the earliest films ever made, with many examples of shots from the cab, from the front of the locomotive and from the lineside. From this point railways have been perennially popular with film makers, and trains play central roles in all kinds of films, from American Westerns to James Bond and Harry Potter. Classic train films include *The General, The Lady Vanishes, Brief Encounter, Oh, Mr Porter!, The Titfield Thunderbolt, Murder on the Orient Express, The Railway Children* and many, many more. There is also a vast library of promotional and enthusiasts' films, quantities of which are now vital historical documents. Many films and television programmes have railway settings, often created in the studio. However, real settings and real stations, particularly on quieter lines, have regularly been used. Recently the task of the film maker and TV producer has been greatly eased by the proliferation of preserved steam railways which, with their collections of ancient locomotives, vehicles and railway relics make ideal settings for period dramas.

▲ Schoolchildren chat to the driver and fireman of British Railways B1 class locomotive no. 61253 at Shenfield Station, Essex, in a scene from British Transport Films *To Norwich and the Norfolk Broads*, a typical promotional production of the 1950s.

◀▼ The Beatles film *A Hard Day's Night*, directed by Richard Lester (1964), was partly filmed on location at Minehead station, in Somerset, the terminus of a long branch line from Taunton and now the home of the West Somerset Railway. These amateur photographs of John looking tired (below), Paul and a friend with teddy bear (lower left), and Paul, George and Ringo, with Wilfred Brambell in the background (top left), were taken during the filming.

▶ This is a scene from *Chariots of Fire*, the famous film about British athletes and the 1924 Olympics. The locomotive starring in the shot is the South Eastern & Chatham Railway's no. 737, built in Ashford in 1901 and now part of the National Collection at the Railway Museum in York. The setting is York station, an unlikely place to find a locomotive from the south of England in 1924. Historical blunders of this kind are very common.

◀ In May 1983 actors and a film crew from BBC Wales are hard at work making *The Fasting Girl*, a typical TV period drama. The setting is Arley station on the preserved Severn Valley Railway, but for the purposes of the film it is Pencader, on a rural line in west Wales. Stations and trains, as well as actors, often take on different roles.

STATION SIGNS

The wonderful diversity of signs and notices issued by the various companies is part of the appeal of railway history, and certainly attracts collectors today. For much of the Victorian period cast iron and wood were used universally, but every railway managed to develop its own look or style. Particularly distinctive were the styles developed by the Big Four companies from the 1920s. Later, the emphasis switched to enamel, and signs in this material dominated the 20th century. Other materials to be found included cast concrete, ceramic tiles and printed tin. Most were factory made but plenty of hand-painted versions for local use were also produced. Metal signs, particularly iron, are very durable and many old signs were still to be seen around the network well into the 1980s. When British Railways was formed, its managers immediately addressed the issue of a national house style that could be applied universally. Letter forms were standardized but more significant was the emergence from the late 1940s of the famous 'double sausage' totem symbol and its regional colours, merging past and present into a modern look.

▲ Free-standing name boards were made by many companies in many styles, usually from wood, sometimes with iron letters, or cast concrete. This is an LSWR one from Devon.

▲ In the 1930s the Southern Railway developed its famous target-style enamel station signs, perhaps inspired by the London Transport roundel. Many survived into the 1950s and 60s, such as this one from Dorset.

◄▲ From the earliest days railways were concerned about the risks run by people who wandered on to the tracks, so all companies erected metal 'Trespass' signs such as the Victorian Taff Vale example photographed in situ in the 1950s (left). Even more common were the 'Beware of Trains' signs (above) by every crossing and on most platforms.

◄ This 1920s enamel sign from Castle Howard, in Yorkshire, was saved when the station closed. These larger, longer signs, sometimes known as running-in boards, were set at the platform ends to be legible from moving trains.

DURHAM

North Eastern Region

FORT WILLIAM

Scottish Region

GRIMSBY TOWN

Eastern Region

NOTTINGHAM
MIDLAND

London Midland Region

TILEHURST

Western Region

CLAPHAM JUNCTION

Southern Region

▲ In the late 1940s British Railways created its famous totem symbol and began to apply it throughout the network. At the same time, the various regional colours, as seen above, were established, along with detailed rules about the design and use on all signs and publicity.

Totems and their associated colours were used until the 1960s and were then gradually replaced. Some survived into the 1970s, while other coloured signs lived on longer, well into the 1990s. All are now keenly collected by rail enthusiasts, and replicas are made. .

PLEASE SHOW TICKETS

◀ The totem style and lettering and the regional colours were applied to enamel notices all over the British Railways network.

▲ The GWR modernization programme of the 1930s made much use of ceramic tiles for signs. This example is at Exeter St David's.

WESTERN **BRITISH RAILWAYS** REGION

HOLIDAY RUNABOUT TICKETS

ISSUED ON ANY DAY FROM
27th APRIL to 25th OCTOBER, 1958
Available for ONE WEEK from date of issue
PROVIDE
UNLIMITED TRAVEL IN HOLIDAY AREAS
CORNISH RIVIERA, GLORIOUS DEVON
and SMILING SOMERSET

SECOND CLASS FARES

Areas Nos. 1, 2, 3, 4, 5, 6, 7, 11, 20 and 21	**18s. 6d.** each	Areas Nos. 3A, 4A and 20A	**26s. 0d.** each
		Area No. 6A	**29s. 0d.**
Area No. 1A	**24s. 6d.**	Area No. 7A	**31s. 0d.**
Children under Three years of age, Free ; Three years and under Fourteen years of age, Half-fare.			

CORNISH RIVIERA—Areas Nos. 1 and 1A.

Tickets are also issued including trips on River Fal vessels of Enterprise Pleasure Cruises Ltd. at an additional charge of 6s. 0d. 2nd class (Area No. 1a)

◀ This British Railways 1958 'Holiday Runabout' leaflet shows how the totem symbol was universally applied from the late 1940s until its replacement in the 1960s by new BR house styles.

AT WAR

OFF TO WAR

In 1918 General Ludendorff stated, as Germany faced defeat: 'There comes a time when locomotives are more important than guns', and certainly the British government understood the strategic importance of an efficient railway network. Transportation of troops and supplies around the country and to embarkation ports was the primary concern and a series of Victorian Acts of Parliament gave the government increasing powers over the railways in times of emergency. These were not fully used until World War I, when a Railway Executive Committee took control of the network. The demands made on the system were extreme, but the railways coped. Apart from the timetabled services and troop movements to and from the ports, the railways ran a vast range of special services, for example 13,630 coal trains from south Wales to Scotland to supply the navy during the war. The Committee took over again in 1939 and faced even greater problems, with the additional burden of damage caused by air raids and, in 1940, the risk of invasion. As in World War I, many railway employees joined the forces and railway workshops made tanks, guns and ammunition. The supreme test was Operation Overlord in 1944 and, as always, the railways delivered the goods.

◀ All the Big Four railway companies issued books and pamphlets describing their contribution to the war effort. This is the Southern Railway's version, issued in 1946.

▲ During World War II around 250,000 special trains carried troops and equipment, all requiring detailed planning to operate smoothly on the network alongside the regular timetabled services. For some, such as the 620 trains needed to move the 300,000 troops saved from Dunkirk, there was no time to plan, but still the trains got through.

▲ The strategic importance of the railways was fully demonstrated by their role in World War I, primarily as troop carriers. Here, a group of soldiers pose at Barnstaple Town, perhaps after attending a training course.

◀ An evocative scene at a station somewhere in Britain as troops in full combat equipment snatch a moment for a breather and a cigarette before their journey continues, perhaps to an embarkation port.

► A popular event on many preserved lines is a World War II re-enactment day, when trains, stations and people turn back the clock in the most detailed way. Here, on the South Devon Railway in the late 1990s, the Home Guard of the 1940s comes back to life, in a scene reminiscent of the BBC's *Dad's Army*.

► In the spring of 1940 a German invasion of Britain seemed highly likely, so frantic preparations were undertaken to train both regular soldiers and the Home Guard in resistance techniques. The railways were a vital strategic resource and exercises were carried out to develop ways of protecting their infrastructure.

THE BLITZ

The railway network was a natural target and German bombers did their best to bring it to a standstill. Through World War II there were over 10,000 attacks on the railways and between 1940 and 1942 severe damage was caused almost on a daily, or rather, nightly basis. Stations and other railway buildings were hit, bridges, viaducts, junctions and signalling were damaged or destroyed, and services were regularly interrupted. However, in most cases the damage was quickly repaired. During the famous raid on Coventry on 14 November 1940, 122 railway installations were damaged, with one 3-mile section of line receiving 40 direct hits. Yet before the end of the month everything was back to normal. Near London, one 2-mile stretch of line was attacked 92 times in nine months. This was the pattern throughout the country but, thanks to adequate preparation, skilled engineering, improvisation and the dedication of the staff, the trains usually kept running, despite serious manpower shortages and problems caused by the blackout.

▲ Paddington's post office and booking office were hit by a German bomb on 17 April 1941. All London's main stations were attacked but none were permanently closed. Inevitably London and the south-east of England fared the worst: the Southern Railway experienced 170 incidents for every 100 miles of route.

▶ During World War II many stations were damaged, especially around London, and railways were regularly attacked in the hope that lines of communication would be cut. This scene of devastation greeted staff at London's St Pancras after a raid in 1942. Within days things were back to normal.

STATION SCULPTURE

ANY OF THOSE associated with the building and running of railways are commemorated by statues and memorials. Stephenson and Brunel have several, but many lesser figures are also remembered, along with those killed in accidents. Most of these statues and memorials date from the 19th century, a period when sculpture was considered important. Sculpture was commonly associated with architecture, and a number of major city station buildings have significant sculptural decoration. The most striking railway sculptures are war memorials. Thousands of railway employees were killed in both World Wars and their sacrifice is commemorated on stations all over the country. These memorials are usually in the form of plaques listing the names, but at some stations they took the form of major works in bronze or stone by leading artists. There are impressive examples in London, at Euston, at Waterloo, in the form of a Victory Arch, and at Paddington, where C S Jagger's great soldier figure commands platform 1.

▲ Sculptures honouring particular individuals are comparatively rare on stations. This is a relief portrait of J H Renton on Rannoch Moor in Scotland. Renton was a great supporter of this wild and remote line.

▼ Dover Marine station is now a car park but the building survives, along with the magnificent war memorial by W King, a winged Victory commemorating the employees of the SER killed in World War 1.

▲ A few things escaped the wholesale destruction of London's Euston station, notably Baron Carlo Marochetti's large 1870 bronze of Robert Stephenson, now sited outside the new building.

LONDON & NORTH-WESTERN RAILWAY MEMORIAL.
IN GRATEFUL MEMORY OF 3719 MEN OF THE L. & N.-W. RLY. CO.
WHO FOR THEIR COUNTRY, JUSTICE AND FREEDOM SERVED AND DIED
IN THE GREAT WAR, 1914-1919.
THIS MONUMENT WAS RAISED BY THEIR COMRADES AND THE COMPANY
AS A LASTING MEMORIAL TO THEIR DEVOTION.

▲ This postcard commemorates the unveiling by Earl Haig on 21 October 1921 of the memorial to the 3,719 men of the LNWR killed in World War 1. Designed by R Owen, it is a powerful sculpture in the form of an obelisk guarded by four bronze servicemen. It still stands in its original position outside Euston station.

◄ There was always rivalry between the two adjacent stations at Victoria in London, run by different companies, and this was maintained in the rebuilding that took place in the Edwardian era. In 1908 Reginald Blomfield designed a new façade for the South Eastern & Chatham Railway's eastern part of the station. This was a splendidly extravagant, French-style structure in white, highly sculpted Portland stone, complete with paired pediments carried by powerful and bare-chested caryatid figures.

EVACUEES

The plans to evacuate families, and particularly children, from London and other 'front line' towns and cities in the event of war had been drawn up well before the start of World War II and indeed the evacuation actually started on 1 September 1939. Many families and children, and hospital patients, were moved during the next few weeks, but this was merely a rehearsal for the main event, which happened during the summer of 1940, as the Blitz was raging. During that year 805 special trains carried nearly half a million people away from the danger areas, and thousands of city children had to come to terms with separation from their parents in an unfamiliar rural world. Evacuations continued through 1941 but by that time many of the children had returned to their families and the whole experience had become a distant memory. In the summer of 1944, with the arrival of the V1 flying bombs and the V2 rockets, it all started again, and children were once more separated from their families and sent away from London and the Kent coast on special trains. This second evacuation was shortlived and by August it was all over, the V weapon launch sites having been overrun by the Allied armies. The railways were the key to the success of the evacuation plans, and they handled this extra traffic successfully. However, the sight of small children standing on platforms clutching their suitcases and gas masks is one that will never be forgotten.

▲ The bulk of the evacuation traffic was carried by the Southern Railway but all companies played their part. In 1940 the GWR carried 70,000 children in special trains from Paddington, including this group arriving at Maidenhead station. Transport to the London termini and from the destination station to distribution centres in local towns and villages was in fleets of motor buses and coaches. Thanks to careful pre-planning, the whole operation went smoothly, even if many of those taking part did not enjoy it.

◀ Children were evacuated through the autumn of 1939, although the expected aerial bombardment of London and other cities had not happened. This early evacuation, in the event unnecessary, proved to be a vital rehearsal for the real thing in the summer of 1940. Here, children, typically well dressed, are guided on to their train by a policeman on 14 December 1939. For most of them, their stay in the country was to be brief.

▶ By the autumn of 1940 the worst of the Blitz was over but evacuations continued. By now the government had learned that the sight of small children being sent off alone could have a negative effect in propaganda terms, so the mother-and-child scheme was launched. In late September 1940, 3,500 mothers and children left London together. Some of that group are gathered here on the platform, awaiting their train under the watchful eye of the law.

FAREWELLS AND GREETINGS

Throughout World War II timetabled rail services continued to run but journey times were often greatly extended and trains were overcrowded. Blackouts, bombing raids and the threat of gas and chemical attacks made things even worse. Despite the war, many people had to carry on going to school and to work. Some continued to go on outings, or even on holiday, although posters asking 'Is Your Journey Really Necessary?' aimed to restrict train travel by civilians. However, the prime users of the railway network were military personnel, and the trains were vital for transporting troops from all three services to and from their bases and training camps, to and from embarkation ports, and on leave. From the outbreak of war, stations were always crowded with men and women in uniform, and these numbers increased massively after the arrival of Canadians from 1939 and Americans from May 1942. Even in extreme circumstances, the railways always coped, for example in the preparations and run-up to the Normandy landings in 1944. After the landings the burden on the network was just as heavy, and indeed ambulance trains made it heavier. For military personnel, the station was central to their lives at all stages of the war. Every large station was equipped with special support facilities, often run by volunteer organizations, trying to offer comfort and advice to young men and women on extended journeys miles from home. Typical were the WVS mobile canteens serving tea and sandwiches. Daily, at every major station, couples, families and friends were to be seen saying farewell, facing together the uncertainty of long separations overshadowed by the fear of death or injury. At the same time, right beside them, were scenes of joy and happiness as friends, family and loved ones greeted men and women arriving back on leave.

▲ Morale-boosting photographs showing cheerful soldiers on their way to war were part of the government's ceaseless propaganda. This lot, setting off from some city terminus to an unknown future, are doing their best to obey the order to smile merrily.

▲ The journeys were frequently dreadful but at least they were often free or much reduced in cost. Service men and women, and sometimes their families, had access to special leave tickets. This is an LMS third class example issued from Sandhills, in an area of military camps north of Liverpool.

◀ Military personnel arriving in strange cities with time on their hands would head straight for the information boards and kiosks to find food, accommodation or entertainment. Many services clubs were set up close to stations, where men and women could relax in a secure environment. This typical information board was at Glasgow.

▲ World War II was notable for the number of women who served in the army, navy and RAF, as well as the various nursing organizations. They all travelled by train. Here, at some country station, a group of new women recruits, described in the photograph's original caption as 'members of the gentle sex', await the train to their new posting 'somewhere in England'.

▲ In World War I the railways had to cope for the first time with continuous troop movements on a massive scale. This was expected and planned for. However, less anticipated at first was the scale of casualties, resulting in large numbers of ambulance trains running to hospitals all over Britain. Here, nurses and doctors await the arrival of such a train at Hereford.

▶ Sometimes, when arriving at the station on leave or with a few hours to spare before departure, the first thing was to get rid of the heavy kitbag. Railway left-luggage offices often made no charge for military personnel, hence this busy scene where the ladies in civilian clothes have to wait their turn.

MILITARY STATIONS

THE FIRST MILITARY railway was built inside Woolwich Arsenal, the second at Chatham dockyard. From the 1860s networks, both narrow and standard gauge, serving naval dockyards and ordnance depots spread quickly. Some were massive networks. By 1918 Woolwich Arsenal had 120 miles of railway. The rapid expansion of the army volunteer corps from that period also influenced the development of military railways, though for some time regular trains were used for transport to and from the camps, which tended in any case to be temporary. It was in the 1900s, in the build-up towards World War 1, that many permanent camps were established, mostly in Surrey, Hampshire and Wiltshire, notably around Salisbury Plain. Increasingly, these were served by dedicated branch lines with their own stations and infrastructure. The list was substantial by 1914 and included Bisley, Bordon, Bulford, Longmoor, Lydd and Tidworth. Many others were added during World War 1, including now famous names

TIDWORTH BARRACKS, SALISBURY PLAIN.

▲ This Edwardian postcard shows the massive military installation at Tidworth, Wiltshire. Beyond the pony trap, the station, which opened in 1901, is spread across the middle ground, with the camp beyond.

▼ Until World War 1 many army camps relied on regular stations and trains for their troop movements. Here, in 1910, the 4th Somerset Light Infantry, on the way to summer camp, form up on the platform at Lavington, a GWR mainline station east of Westbury, in Wiltshire.

Booking Hall No 2.
Deepcut Camp Station.

▲ Troops parade at Ludgershall, Wiltshire, a public station on the Midland & South Western Junction line north from Andover. However, it had massive sidings and special platforms for military use, and a branch went from here to Tidworth. Today, Ludgershall is a military stores depot, so the line from Andover remains open to serve it, although everything to the north was closed in the 1960s, including the Tidworth branch.

◄ Bisley, in Surrey, was one of the first military stations when it opened in 1890. Later, the branch that served it was extended to Pirbright, Deepcut and Blackdown. This postcard shows the 'other ranks' booking hall at Deepcut Camp station, complete with newsstand.

▲ Until it closed in 1969 the Longmoor Military Railway was famous for its open days. Here, in the late 1960s crowds watch the railway's star, the now preserved 2-10-0 War Department locomotive 'Gordon'.

such as Blandford, Catterick and Pirbright. Still more followed in World War II. In most cases there was a military station at the end of a siding or branch, but sometimes there were complete military networks with several stations, notably Catterick and Longmoor. The latter had 13 stations on its line from Bentley to Liss. At various times there were at least 60 dedicated stations serving army camps, and many others serving naval bases, ordnance depots and military hospitals. There were also navy and air force railways, with their own stations. Some navy railways were in dockyard complexes such as Devonport and Rosyth; others were distinct branch lines, for example those serving Cairnryan, Faslane and Shoeburyness. As for the air force, Cranwell and Manston had their own branch lines, while other airfields, including Finningley, had their own stations. Most military stations disappeared after World War II. Few survive, apart from stores depots such as Bicester and Ludgershall.

London and South Western Ry.
FROM WATERLOO TO
787
BISLEY CAMP

THE FINAL WHISTLE

LAST DAYS

Railways were always subject to the effects of government legislation on all areas of their construction and operation. Before an inch of track could be laid on any railway scheme, a bill had to be presented to both houses of Parliament, to seek government approval and ultimately Royal Assent. Numerous Acts brought into force through the Victorian era impinged directly upon the running of railways; some were in response to safety issues following accidents, others were financial. Through the 19th century there were attempts at devolving powers away from central government but in the end the government could not avoid actions that radically changed the nature of railways in Britain, first through nationalization and then through privatization. Closing a railway was also a complicated process, requiring government approval, with various levels of appeal available to the public. A firm principle was that there had to be an adequate alternative transport system available to the public. Prior to the 1960s, closures usually occurred without a great outcry from the public but all that changed with the Beeching Report of 1963, advocating as it did closures on an unprecedented scale that would directly affect the lives of hundreds of thousands of people. As closure notices went up, so the protests and appeals began and, in some cases, the process of closure took years. However, in the vast majority of cases the British Railways Board eventually had its way and line after line, all over Britain, came to face its final day of operation.

▲ A small crowd on 19 September 1954 bids farewell to the last passenger train on the branch to London's Cystal Palace High Level, the grand station opened in 1854 to serve the relocated 1851 Great Exhibition building.

▼ On 7 September 1963 a Castle class no. 7036 draws the express for Weston-super-Mare into Yatton station on the last day of steam on the route. On the adjacent platform the local for Wells waits to depart on what was also the last day of scheduled services on the famous Cheddar Valley line.

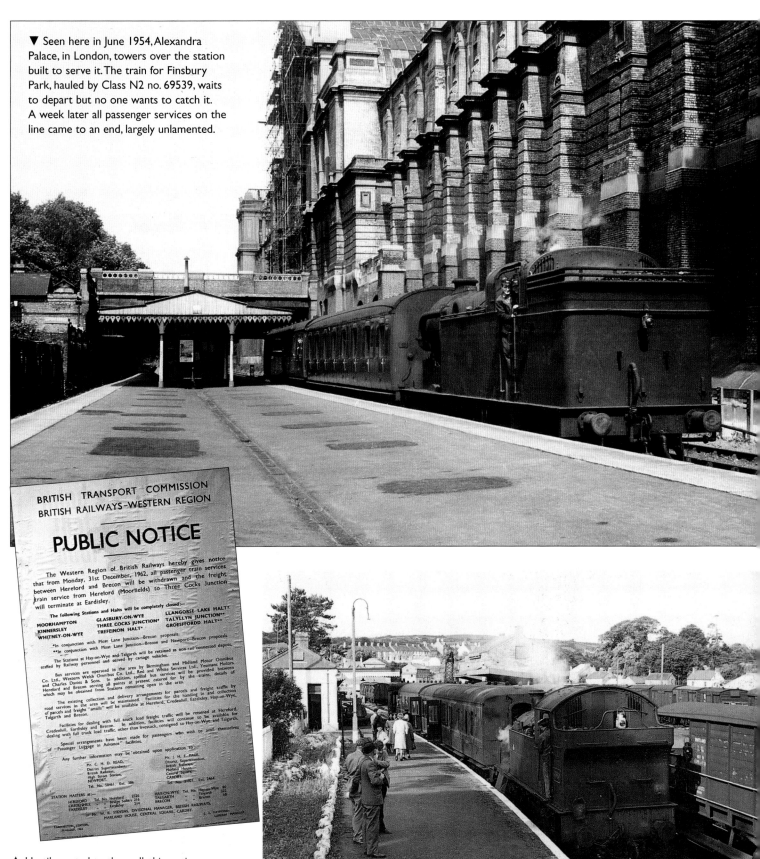

▼ Seen here in June 1954, Alexandra Palace, in London, towers over the station built to serve it. The train for Finsbury Park, hauled by Class N2 no. 69539, waits to depart but no one wants to catch it. A week later all passenger services on the line came to an end, largely unlamented.

BRITISH TRANSPORT COMMISSION
BRITISH RAILWAYS-WESTERN REGION

PUBLIC NOTICE

The Western Region of British Railways hereby gives notice that from Monday, 31st December, 1962, all passenger train services between Hereford and Brecon will be withdrawn and the freight train service from Hereford (Moorfields) to Three Cocks Junction will terminate at Eardisley.

The following Stations and Halts will be completely closed:—

MOORHAMPTON	GLASBURY-ON-WYE	LLANGORSE LAKE HALT*
KINNERSLEY	THREE COCKS JUNCTION	TALYLLYN JUNCTION**
WHITNEY-ON-WYE	TREFEINON HALT*	GROESFFORDD HALT**

*In conjunction with Moat Lane Junction—Brecon proposals.
**In conjunction with Moat Lane Junction—Brecon and Newport—Brecon proposals.

The Stations at Hay-on-Wye and Talgarth will be retained as non-rail connected depots, staffed by Railway personnel and served by cartage vehicles.

Bus services are operated in the area by Birmingham and Midland Motor Omnibus Co. Ltd., Western Welsh Omnibus Co. Ltd., Red and White Services Ltd., Yeomans Motors and Charles Davies & Sons. In addition, special bus services will be provided between Hereford and Brecon serving all points at present catered for by the trains, details of which may be obtained from Stations remaining open in the area.

The existing collection and delivery arrangements for parcels and freight traffic by road services in the area will be maintained. Facilities for the handing in and collection of parcels and freight "smalls" will be available at Hereford, Credenhill, Eardisley, Hay-on-Wye, Talgarth and Brecon.

Facilities for dealing with full truck load freight traffic will be retained at Hereford, Credenhill, Eardisley and Brecon. In addition, facilities will continue to be available for dealing with full truck load traffic, other than livestock, consigned to Hay-on-Wye and Talgarth.

Special arrangements have been made for passengers who wish to avail themselves of "Passenger Luggage in Advance" facilities.

Any further information may be obtained upon application to:—

Mr. C. H. D. READ,
District Superintendent,
British Railways,
High Street Station,
NEWPORT. Tel. No. 58461. Ext. 386

Mr. J. H. E. PAGE,
District Superintendent,
British Railways,
Marland House,
Central Square,
CARDIFF. Tel. No. 31021. Ext. 2464.

STATION MASTERS at. Tel. No. Hereford

HEREFORD	Tel. No. Hereford	2326	HAY-ON-WYE Tel. No. Hay-on-Wye	80
CREDENHILL	Bridge Sollers	216	TALGARTH	312
EARDISLEY	Eardisley	214	BRECON	Brecon

Or Mr. W. R. STEVENS, DIVISIONAL MANAGER, BRITISH RAILWAYS, MARLAND HOUSE, CENTRAL SQUARE, CARDIFF.
S. E. RAYMOND, GENERAL MANAGER.

PADDINGTON, STATION,
November, 1962.

▲ Hastily pasted to the wall, this notice announces the closure, with effect from 31 December 1962, of all passenger services on the line from Hereford to Brecon, along with nine intermediate stations. Within a year, such notices would be appearing thick and fast all over Britain.

▲ A small but well-dressed group has turned out at Cardigan to attend the last day of passenger services, 8 September 1962, on the long branch line from Whitland. Ten years later a similar event would have drawn large crowds.

STEAM EXCURSIONS

THE IDEA OF RUNNING special excursion trains for railway enthusiasts, using historic locomotives and carriages, dates back at least to the 1920s and probably earlier. Initially, these were generally operated to mark important railway anniversaries, such as the railway centenary celebrations of 1925. Later, the locomotives became the focus of attention, with many excursions organized by enthusiasts' societies and clubs. Often these explored complex and convoluted routes that would have been impossible to travel by scheduled services. Sometimes they featured a number of locomotives. Steam excursions became more common in the 1960s, with people increasingly keen to travel routes threatened with closure, often in trains hauled by locomotives destined for extinction. It all came to an end in 1968 and for a while British Rail would not allow steam locomotives to run on its network. Eventually the ban was relaxed, and since the 1970s steam excursions have run in increasing numbers each year, some being so regular they have entered the timetable. Many famous locomotives are licensed to operate these trains, but experienced crews are now harder to find.

▲ On 2 May 1964 crowds came to see the special last train at Brecon station. This was a typical example of the steam excursions that frequently operated over routes about to close.

▼ In May 1973 two famous locomotives, BR 92203 'Black Prince' and GWR 6000 'King George V', draw the crowds at Hereford, then a famous and very active steam centre. Such scenes were commonplace in the early days of steam excursions, but today toleration of this kind of 'pitch invasion' is utterly inconceivable.

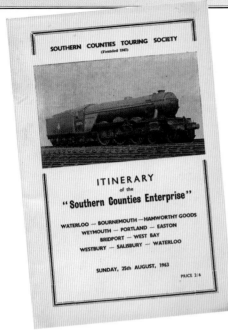

▲ Societies often produced itinerary brochures for their special steam excursions. The Southern Counties Enterprise ran in August 1963 to many remote parts of south-western England.

▼ In 1959 the platform at Birmingham New Street is packed with enthusiasts awaiting the departure of the newly restored Midland Compound no. 1000 at the head of a special.

▲ On 1 May 1968, no. 4472 'Flying Scotsman', newly in private ownership, sets off from Kings Cross to celebrate the 40th anniversary of the inaugural non-stop service of the Flying Scotsman express between London and Edinburgh. This was also a key date in the story of mainline steam excursions, for they then ended for some years. In the foreground is the usual Flying Scotsman service, then hauled by Deltics – which now survive only in preservation.

DERELICTION

Although Dr Beeching is usually blamed for closing much of the railway network – and his report did recommend the closing of 280 lines and 1,850 stations – there have been closures ever since the 19th century. One of the first was in 1833, when the Stockton & Darlington closed its short branch to Yarm. Some longer lines were closed in the 1850s. However, increasingly complicated government legislation, regularly amended and updated through the Victorian period, controlled the process of closure, while other laws governed the abandonment of railway schemes never built or completed. As a result, closures were relatively rare, and by about 1920 a total of only 400 miles of railway had been closed, nearly a quarter of which were in Scotland. The 1923 Grouping into four major railway operating companies coincided with a steady increase in competition from road transport, notably goods vehicles and motor buses. The Big Four responded by becoming more efficient and cost-conscious and by running their own fleets of motor vehicles. They also instigated a wider-ranging programme of line closures, which concentrated on duplicated routes and loss-making branch lines. Between 1923 and 1947 over 1,600 miles of railway were closed, 20 per cent of which were in Scotland. The longest individual line was the 36 miles from Coldstream to Alnwick, typical of the rural routes that were hardest hit. When British Railways was formed, the pattern continued and a further

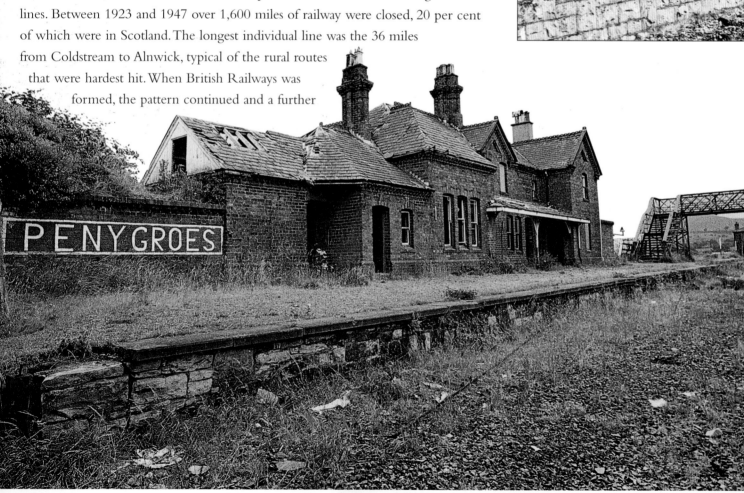

▲ The tracks have gone but the GWR name board remains as dereliction takes hold at Sandford & Banwell, a station on the Cheddar line between Wells and Yatton. This pretty stone-built, cottage-style station had extravagant bargeboarding and patterned roof tiles, and its own goods shed.

▶ The Great Western built a new station at Birmingham in 1912, at Snow Hill. A large and efficiently planned building, it was highly regarded at the time. In 1972 it was taken out of use and largely abandoned, becoming for a while an unofficial car park, as this photograph indicates. Soon afterwards it was demolished, a short-sighted act typical of its time. In 1987 a new Snow Hill was opened on the site, to relieve congestion at New Street.

◀ The Afonwen to Caernarfon line in north Wales was closed in 1964 but in 1970 there was still plenty to be seen at Penygroes, including the substantial station buildings, the iron lattice footbridge and the signal box. This was the junction station for the Nantlle branch, closed by the LMS in 1932.

▲ Another 1960s loss was Winchester's second station, Chesil (or Cheesehill), the end of the line for the GWR route from Newbury. For a while the French-style station buildings survived, set dramatically at the mouth of a tunnel, but the site has since been cleared.

► Morecambe had two stations, the grander of which was Promenade, built by the Midland Railway in 1907. This was a big, handsome terminus in a kind of Gothic style, with a massive glazed concourse and decorative tiling. In 1994 it was replaced by a new station nearer the town centre and it was disused when photographed in 1995. It now has a new life as an information and leisure centre.

▲ Nothing better expresses the romance of the derelict station than this view of Petworth, a station on the line that linked Pulborough and Midhurst in Sussex. An intrepid explorer makes his way through the jungle in 1979, long after the station was closed. Long-term survival of this kind is unusual and in this case it enabled the station to be restored later as a house.

1,250 miles were closed between 1948 and 1953. Also accelerated was the removal of passenger services, leaving lines open only for goods traffic. This affected a further 1,100 miles during the same period.

Dr Richard Beeching became chairman of the British Railways Board in 1962 and proceeded to analyse the cost-effectiveness of the network on a line by line and station by station basis, something that had never been done before. His report, based on his findings, recommended the closure of thousands of miles of railway all over Britain, much of which was subsequently carried out under the auspices of both Conservative and Labour governments. The bulk of the closures occurred in the 1960s and by 1975 it was all over. The legacy of this ten-year closure period was thousands of miles of abandoned trackbed and many more thousands of abandoned stations, railway buildings, bridges, tunnels and associated structures. Some were demolished, some were acquired for other purposes but the majority,

◄ Passenger trains ceased to run to Dungeness from Lydd Junction, in Kent, in 1937, and the rest of the lines that ran towards the coast from Appledore were closed in the 1950s and 1960s. However, Dungeness station lingered on for years, isolated in the vast Romney Marsh landscape. Today, trains are running again, servicing the nuclear power station.

► Withington, on the M&SWJ line from Cheltenham to Andover, was a pre-Beeching closure. Traffic ceased in 1961 and by the summer of 1963 contractors were on the site, removing the track and anything worth salvaging. Work seems to be proceeding in a rather leisurely manner, in a setting that shows Gloucestershire at its best.

▼ East Anglia suffered during the Beeching era and among the losses was most of the old Midland & Great Northern network. Gedney was an M&GN station, a surprisingly large structure for this small town east of Spalding. Remarkably, plenty survives, as this recent photograph shows, with plenty of potential for development.

particularly those in the countryside, were simply left to moulder away. Many have subsequently vanished, others have been given a new life in various ways, but even today derelict stations and station buildings are still occasionally to be found, often as ruins picturesquely overgrown and hidden in remote spots. However, the heyday for dereliction was in the 1960s and 1970s, with thousands of former stations still standing, and still recognizable, to be discovered and explored in every part of Britain. The lost station, and its lost lines, became in this period a favourite subject for photographers both professional and amateur; the first books on the subject appeared in the 1960s, a striking reflection of the romantic love of dereliction and decay that is so much a part of the British character.

▲ The line from Peterhead to Maud Junction was closed in 1965 but there is still plenty to be seen, including long-abandoned and overgrown Mintlaw station. At one time this stone building was known by the delightful name of Old Deer & Mintlaw.

WHY DID WE GO THERE?

THURSO, right at the very top of Britain, received its railway connection in 1874, at the same time as its near neighbour Wick, and these two remote destinations, served by the same train from Inverness, have always been partners. Thurso, which is the harbour for Orkney and the Shetland Islands, is set among the wild cliffs that mark mainland Britain's most northerly coast. It and its surroundings offer visitors all the true pleasures of the most remote areas of Scotland.

(A. 398)

THE HIGHLAND RAILWAY.

LUGGAGE.

From _FORRES_

To THURSO

Royal Burgh of

WICK

OFFICIAL GUIDE BOOK

▲ Set on a river estuary, a one-time major fishing port and a royal burgh since 1589, Wick has long appealed to visitors.

▲ Lerwick is the capital of Shetland, long accessible from Thurso by regular ferry services, so it has always enjoyed visitors seeking a lifestyle very different from the British mainland. The 1950s visitor who sent this postcard also enjoyed 'hot and sunny weather'.

► The pleasures, and pitfalls, of fly fishing had always brought visitors to Scotland. The railway to Thurso opened up remote rivers and lochs and brought many newcomers to the sport.

Highland Hut

A Highland Piper

◀ The railway to Thurso and Wick brought about a greater appreciation of the Highland life destroyed by the Clearances of the Victorian era. Though romantic, Edwardian cards such as this showed what had been lost, and the culture that had been destroyed.

▶ The railways to the Highlands in the Victorian era encouraged the interest among visitors in Scottish traditions. Tartan became very fashionable among those who followed the royal lead.

DUNCANSBAY HEAD, JOHN 'O' GROATS.

▲ Duncansby Head, with its towering 200ft cliffs and famous lighthouse, has always attracted visitors. A sailor, about to set off from Thurso, sent this card to his daughter in 1944.

▶ St Magnus's cathedral in Kirkwall, the capital of Orkney, dates back to the 12th century. Kirkwall is a short ferry trip from Thurso harbour.

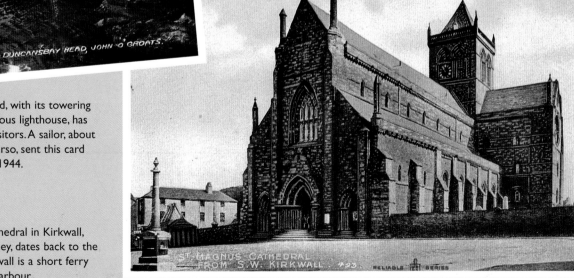

ST. MAGNUS CATHEDRAL
FROM S.W. KIRKWALL. 423.   RELIABLE SERIES

A NEW LIFE

Following the closure of a railway line there is a period when not much happens. This may last for weeks, months, or even years. Then salvage gangs arrive, either railway employees or independent contractors, to remove the track and its associated metalwork, the sleepers, the signalling equipment, lighting and signage and other portable parts of the infrastructure. Engineers may then remove metal bridges and other major structures such as station canopies and train shed roofs. At this stage the smaller buildings tend to survive, but face an uncertain future. The trackbed may be sold off piecemeal, for agriculture, for housing, for industry or for new roads, but many of the buildings and structures are left to decay quietly. Practical buildings such as goods sheds and warehouses are frequently taken over by new owners and put to use, but more durable structures like bridges and tunnels may stay in that state of gentle dereliction for years. Stations and houses

▶ When it was completed in 1880 Manchester Central boasted the second widest single-span, cast-iron arch in Britain (the widest being St Pancras, which it closely resembles). It was used jointly by three railways, the Midland, the Great Northern and the Great Central. Closed in 1969, it lingered for years like a stranded whale in Mosley Street. Then in 1986 it was sensitively and imaginatively converted into the G-Mex, Greater Manchester Exhibition and Event Centre, a role it fulfils excellently. As this 1995 photo shows, it is served by Manchester's tram network.

▶ The Strathpeffer branch near Inverness was in operation from 1885 to 1951. Despite this early closure, Strathpeffer station survived and now houses a craft centre, café and museum of childhood.

▲ As a station, Darras Hall, a stop on a colliery branch near Ponteland, north-east of Newcastle, had a short life in the 1920s. However, the timber station building survived and in 1963 became a Presbyterian church, seen here in June 1973.

▼ One of Scotland's most remote railways was the Dornoch branch, which closed in 1960. Much of the route can still be traced through glorious scenery. Tangible remains include Skelbo platform and station house, the latter much enlarged as a private house.

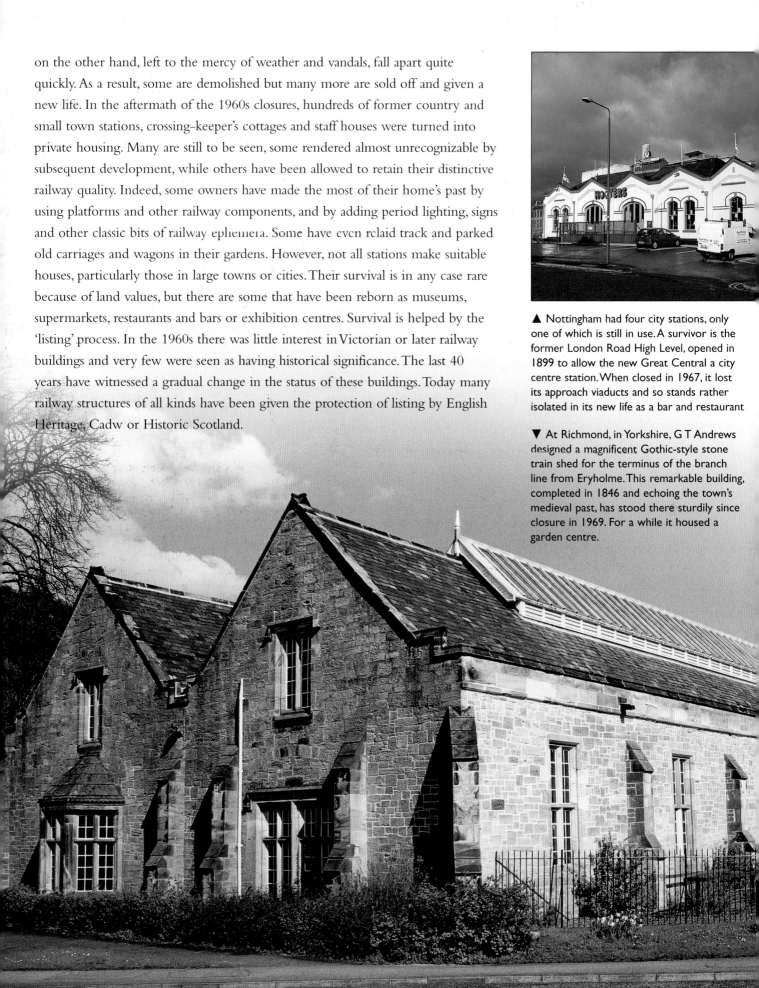

on the other hand, left to the mercy of weather and vandals, fall apart quite quickly. As a result, some are demolished but many more are sold off and given a new life. In the aftermath of the 1960s closures, hundreds of former country and small town stations, crossing-keeper's cottages and staff houses were turned into private housing. Many are still to be seen, some rendered almost unrecognizable by subsequent development, while others have been allowed to retain their distinctive railway quality. Indeed, some owners have made the most of their home's past by using platforms and other railway components, and by adding period lighting, signs and other classic bits of railway ephemera. Some have even relaid track and parked old carriages and wagons in their gardens. However, not all stations make suitable houses, particularly those in large towns or cities. Their survival is in any case rare because of land values, but there are some that have been reborn as museums, supermarkets, restaurants and bars or exhibition centres. Survival is helped by the 'listing' process. In the 1960s there was little interest in Victorian or later railway buildings and very few were seen as having historical significance. The last 40 years have witnessed a gradual change in the status of these buildings. Today many railway structures of all kinds have been given the protection of listing by English Heritage, Cadw or Historic Scotland.

▲ Nottingham had four city stations, only one of which is still in use. A survivor is the former London Road High Level, opened in 1899 to allow the new Great Central a city centre station. When closed in 1967, it lost its approach viaducts and so stands rather isolated in its new life as a bar and restaurant

▼ At Richmond, in Yorkshire, G T Andrews designed a magnificent Gothic-style stone train shed for the terminus of the branch line from Eryholme. This remarkable building, completed in 1846 and echoing the town's medieval past, has stood there sturdily since closure in 1969. For a while it housed a garden centre.

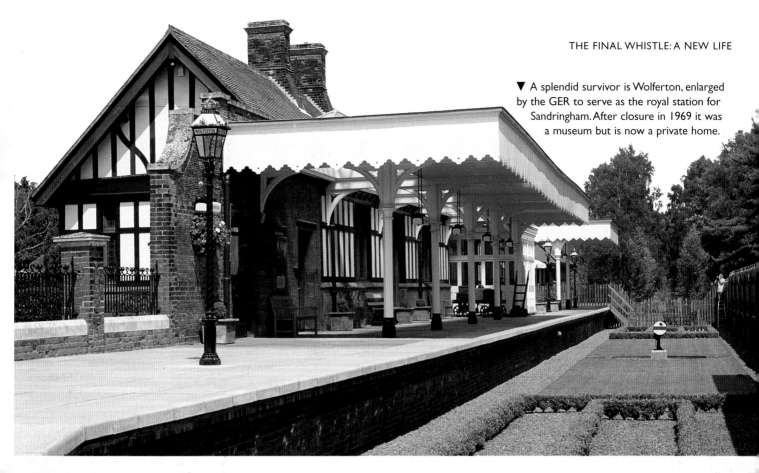

▼ A splendid survivor is Wolferton, enlarged by the GER to serve as the royal station for Sandringham. After closure in 1969 it was a museum but is now a private home.

◀ After a long period of decay and dereliction, Petworth, a former London, Brighton & South Coast station in Sussex, has been brought back to life as a private house, complete with platform and bridge.

▼ There are many ways to convert a station into a house while retaining the flavour of the original, but quite common is the idea of turning the trackbed between the platforms into a sunken garden. This is Daggons Road, formerly an intermediate stop on the old LSWR line that wandered through Wiltshire and Dorset from Salisbury to Wimborne.

STATION ART

ALTHOUGH STATIONS have from the earliest days been essentially functional structures, their design and decoration often reflected the artistic ambitions of their creators. In the Victorian era decoration was mostly in stone, brick and iron, but colourful tiling and stained glass were not uncommon. Later, pictures, generally promotional, were hung in public areas such as waiting and refreshment rooms. However, the idea of actually applying art to the walls of station buildings did not fully emerge until the late 20th century. The last years of British Rail were marked by a number of decorative painting, tiling and sculptural schemes, sometimes in conjunction with local art colleges. There have also been some endearing but largely amateur projects, usually involving supporters of a particular line or station.

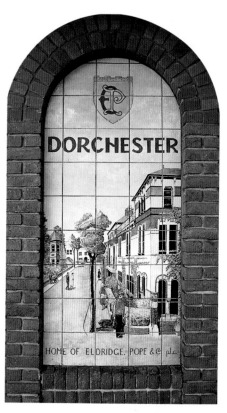

▲ Dorchester South station was rebuilt in 1986. The involvement of the local brewer, Eldridge Pope, is acknowledged in two tile panels on the new building. One shows Dorchester's High Street and the other (above) part of the brewery buildings.

◀ The covered footbridge at Southampton Central station features a dynamic mosaic mural inspired by shipping and the port. It was designed in 1990 by Sue Ridge.

▲ In Stoke-on-Trent station the subway is enlivened by a colourful tile mural featuring many aspects of the city's history: potteries and their ovens and products, coal mining, canals, football and the railways. Designed by local artist Liz Kayley, who worked with 200 local children, it was unveiled on 18 October 1994.

▶ In the 1980s the main staircase at Exeter St David's was decorated with a series of murals in the style of the Renaissance depicting modern railway life. Truly wonderful and eccentric, they are not now being cared for and the artist's name panel has vanished, along with its dedication: 'Thanks to Michelangelo and British Rail'.

◀ A dull concrete wall on Wrabness station, on the Harwich branch, has been transformed by a delightful mural of waiting passengers painted in a lively, primitive manner with beautifully observed detail.

NEW AND REBUILT STATIONS

There is a kind of life cycle that can be applied to a station. When a line was originally being planned and built, the location and scale of the stations along its route was determined by cost and by anticipated traffic. The latter, assessed by rather crude methods and overlaid with a strong helping of optimism, often tended to be wrong, despite the great celebrations that usually accompanied the opening of a new railway. Many stations were too big, and never fulfilled the dreams of those that encouraged and paid for them. Others were too small, and had rapidly to be rebuilt or enlarged. Some were simply in the wrong place. When traffic patterns had stabilized, most stations could look forward to a period of settled maturity, interrupted only by routine maintenance or repairs. When maintenance costs were deemed to be excessive or the buildings too old-fashioned or impractical, stations were sometimes rebuilt on the same site, usually in a more modern style. Railway companies have always been image conscious, so have wanted to be seen as modern – in their buildings as much as their trains. Busy stations were therefore constantly altered and improved, often in a piecemeal manner.

▲ On 9 March 1899, the crowds gathered to celebrate the Great Central Railway's opening of Brackley station, in Northamptonshire. Dignitaries and officials mixed with locals on the unfinished platform, while children enjoyed a day off school. Even at this late date, station openings were grand occasions, marked by speeches, flags and bunting, brass bands and plenty of food and drink. No one seems to mind that the place is still a building site.

◀ The end of the 19th century witnessed a massive growth in commuter traffic in cities all over Britain, resulting in an ever-increasing demand for more trains and bigger stations. This was greater in London than anywhere else, forcing well-established companies such as the LSWR, the Great Eastern and the SECR to turn themselves into efficient operators of commuter services. This photograph of a station somewhere in south London shows new buildings under construction.

▶ This photograph shows Brighouse station under construction in 2000, a classic case of the railway responding to changing social needs. The old Victorian station at Brighouse had closed in 1970, but 30 years later it was needed again as a stop on the route from York to Manchester via Huddersfield.

Next came a period of decline, usually slow but irreversible. Staff were reduced, regular maintenance was abandoned, buildings were demolished or left empty. In some cases, all the buildings were removed, leaving only bare platforms and a primitive shelter. When a line closed, the prospect for the stations was gloomy: abandonment and decay, demolition or, very occasionally, change of use. In rare cases, the line reopened as a preserved railway and the cycle went into reverse, with stations rebuilt as glorious evocations of their former selves, or created from scratch.

While there have been station closures since the earliest days of the railways, there has also been a long history of new stations being added to the network, inspired usually by changing social patterns such as the building of new towns and new estates, the setting up of new industries, the opening of shopping centres, airports or leisure and sporting centres. In a few cases, in response to changing local needs, long-closed lines and long-abandoned stations have been brought back into use and added to the national network. From the 1960s many stations were in decline because of a lack of investment and a general disregard of anything to do with railways and their history, prompting in many cases unnecessary alterations or demolition. Since then, a greater understanding of the importance of railway buildings in heritage terms has resulted in a significant number being listed, and many others being restored with great care. As the country that invented the railway, Britain has a particular responsibility towards the architectural legacy of the railway age. In the maintenance of this legacy, stations are the front line.

▲▶ A classic case of doing the wrong thing: the demolition of Oban's fine wooden Arts & Crafts station of 1880, the proud terminus of the Callander & Oban Railway's line. Its tall, French-style clock tower was a much-loved local landmark and the glazed concourse was always popular with passengers seeking shelter while waiting for ferries. It was, apparently, in good condition, so the demolition in March 1987 seems to have been completely unjustified. The clock tower, still standing amid the debris (above), could easily have been saved. The new station (right) is a mean and unsuitable structure in brick, offering neither style nor shelter.

▲ Thanks to a total restoration in 2000, Bournemouth – formerly Central – station is now back to its 1888 splendour. After a long period of decline, the station seemed likely to lose its roof, and possibly its flanking walls, in order to save maintenance costs. As it is one of the best glazed trainsheds in Britain, that would have been a tragedy. Luckily, attitudes towards such buildings changed significantly during the 1990s and Railtrack bravely took the expensive decision to undertake full restoration of the station.

► After a long period of closure, Llantwit Major station, on the coastal route from Cardiff to Bridgend, reopened and rejoined the national network in 2005. A number of factors influenced the decision to reopen the line, not least the presence of Cardiff airport, now served by Rhoose station.

WISH YOU WERE HERE!
SCOTLAND

*U*NTIL THE COMING *of the railways much of Scotland, apart from the big cities, was remote and inaccessible. The nature of the landscape made great demands on the railway builders but, as the network spread, so trade flourished. More significant was the development of tourism in Scotland, thanks entirely to the railway. Postcards sent by locals as well as visitors celebrate both the landscape and the engineering achievements that carried the railways across the country. The quality of much of the station architecture is a reflection of a justifiable sense of pride, evident in many of the images.*

▶ *Dalmeny ,on the south bank of the Firth of Forth, was originally served by a branch line. However, everything changed with the opening of the Forth Bridge in 1890 and Dalmeny acquired a new mainline station, seen here on this card, with the bridge in the distance. Posted in 1920, the card carries a very typical messsage: 'arrived here Tuesday 7.30am, some journey.'*

Dalmeny Station, South Queensferry.

The Railway Station, Perth.

◀ *Always a busy station and the meeting point for several lines, Perth was regularly enlarged and rebuilt. The 1911 rebuilding created this large and elegant concourse with its glazed roof, decorative clock and displays of flowers and greenery. Judging by the ladies' costumes, this card must have been issued soon after the building works had been finished.*

◀ The most famous disaster in British railway history was the collapse of the bridge across the Tay in December 1879. A new bridge opened ten years later, the longest rail bridge in Britain. This card of about 1910 shows little Wormit station, not much more than a halt at the bridge's southern end, on the loop line to Tayport.

GLASGOW (CENTRAL). NEW PORTION–COAST TRAIN ARRIVING.

▶ This card, posted in 1906, is entitled 'Glasgow Central, New Portion – Coast Train Arriving'. After decades of muddle and confusion, Glasgow Central was rebuilt in 1905, becoming spacious and efficient, as the card indicates, with plenty of room for cabs and passengers. The message is to the point: 'Isn't this a champion station.'

◀ Lenzie was a junction station north-east of Glasgow serving trains on three routes. Typically Scottish is the elegant iron footbridge. This postcard, posted in 1910, has an intriguing message from JB to Miss Reekie: 'Do you recognize anybody standing on the station?' And a male passenger is marked with an X – perhaps the sender of the card?

INDEX

AUTHOR'S ACKNOWLEDGEMENTS

Photographs used in this book have come from many sources. Some have been supplied by photographers or picture libraries, while others have been bought on the open market. In the latter case, photographers or libraries have been acknowledged whenever possible. However, many such images inevitably remain anonymous, despite attempts at tracing or identifying their origin. If photographs or images have been used without due credit or acknowledgement, through no fault of our own, apologies are offered. If you believe this is the case, please let us know as we would like to give full credit in any future edition.

For special help in tracking down rare or unusual images, and for being generous with items from their own collections, thanks are due to Godfrey and Janet Croughton, John and Vivien Forster, Tony Harden, Brian Harding and Somerset Railwayana, Nigel Maddock and Solent Railwayana Auctions, Edwin Phelps and Andrew Swift.

That *Tickets Please!* passed so smoothly from original concept to completed book was due entirely to three people: Sue Gordon, the book's editor, Julian Holland, designer, picture researcher and fellow railway enthusiast, and Mic Cady, commissioning editor at David & Charles. Together and separately they offered enthusiasm and support at all times, not only making the book happen, but also making it fun to do. For unfailing patience, enthusiasm and support of another kind, I am deeply grateful to Chrissie, my wife.

PICTURE CREDITS

Unless otherwise specified, all archive photographs and ephemera are from either the author's or the publisher's collection.

l = left; r = right; t = top; b = bottom; m = middle

Photographs by Paul Atterbury:
6b; 13m; 15bl; 15br; 17tr; 20b; 21bl; 22tr; 22b; 42/43b; 77br; 106b; 142/143t; 155r; 172/173b; 175mr; 185tr; 187tr; 210tr; 210bl; 211br; 219bl; 240/241b; 241ml; 242/243b; 244tr; 244ml; 245br; 248/249t

Other photographs are by:

Anderson, D A: 87t
Ashworth, Ben: 12tr; 16/17b; 27; 45; 48tr; 65bl; 67tr; 67br; 101; 125t; 132b; 148bl; 149br; 150/151b; 159t; 180/181t; 194tr; 195ml; 196b; 229bl; 230b; 237t
Ballantyne, D H: 228b
Ballantyne, Hugh: 11tl; 15tl; 15tr; 60tr; 65br; 74b; 75t; 84bl; 168tr; 184/185b; 193tr; 195tr; 208b; 219tl
Burges, A W: 122/123t
Canning, D E: 44tr; 121b
Carpenter, R: 142ml
Casserley, H C: 112/113b; 114b; 118tl
Coles, C R L: 19m; 228tr; 229t
Connolly, K: 130/131b
Cross, Derek: 102/103b

Dunnett, M: 130bl
Esau, Mike: 6/7b; 55br; 97br; 158b; 176/177; 232b; 233br
Fowler, P J: 56/57b; 57br; 144/145
Gifford, C T: 65tl
Glover, J G: 64tr; 86b
Goss, John: 14br; 124/125b
Griffiths, N. D.: 56/57t
Hall, Colin: 243bl
Harden, Tony: 24bl; 25m; 46bl; 47tl; 47mr; 47bl; 78bl; 81bl; 109br; 110mr; 110bl; 111tl; 111mr; 111bl; 133br; 163tl; 163mr; 163bl; 169bl; 180bl; 184t; 191tr; 199tl; 199mr; 199bl; 250mr; 250bl; 251tl; 251mr; 251bl
Heavyside, G T: 70tr
Heiron, G F: 54b; 58b
Holland, Julian: title page; 4/5b; 5br; 6t; 19br; 25t; 77t; 108b; 109t; 134/135t; 135b; 138/139b; 140/141b; 142/143b; 167tl; 170ml; 171t; 171br; 190/191b; 193b; 194br; 197tr; 200b; 206bl; 210mr; 211ml; 215tr; 236bl; 245t; 248br
Humm, Robert: 23br
Huntriss, Derek: 138tl; 146/147b
Jarvis, Alan: 6tr; 8/9; 14tr; 21t; 23m; 26b; 28tr; 29t; 43r; 52/53; 66b; 107t; 115t; 119t; 122/123b; 132/133t; 134bl; 150tr; 151t; 170tr; 185mr; 188/189b; 194bl; 205tr; 205bl; 206/207b; 210ml; 226/227; 230tr; 249br
Joanes, R N: 229br
Kerr, W D L: 189br
King, M A: 16tr
Lakin, T: 139t

Locomotive & General: 100t; 165br; 170b
Mensing, Michael: 28b; 48b; 55t; 66tr; 96/97t; 128/129b; 178/179b; 186/187b; 231b; 234/235t
Meredith, John: 129mr
Morrison, Gavin: 11b; 13br; 20tr; 21br; 23tr; 34tr; 75br; 91b; 98/99b; 100br; 102/103t; 118b; 126/127t; 127tr; 147br; 168mr; 180/181b; 187tl; 195tl; 196tr; 205tl; 218tr; 234/235b; 240/241t; 244/245b; 247br; 248ml
Mortimer, G R: 64br; 231tr
Oakfield Films: 60/61b
Peters, Ivo, Collection: 44br; 201tl
Photomatic: 26tr
Riley, R C: 12b; 17m; 44bl; 84/85t; 88b; 112/113t; 116/117t; 123br; 195br; 218b; 232/233t
Science & Society Photo Library: 39r; 78/79b; 79tr; 79b; 167m; 174b; 175t; 175br; 208tr; 209br; 216/217; 220tr; 220bl; 221
Scrace, John: 18b
Sharpe, Brian: 14bl; 99t; 192b; 236/237b; 242tr; 243t; 243ml
Swift, Andrew: 10tr; 10b; 36bl; 36mr; 37bl; 40bl; 50b; 51t; 51bl; 59br; 71t; 72/73b; 73t; 80mr; 81mr; 96b; 109ml; 113br; 117b; 120tr; 121tr; 126tl; 126b; 150bl; 160bl; 162bl; 164b; 166bl; 190b; 197br; 198bl; 212/213; 214/215b; 216bl; 223ml; 224b; 225t; 225ml; 246/247t
Thompson, Douglas: 67mr; 115b
Wise, Revd Graham E: 146/147t;

CHAPTER OPENER ILLUSTRATIONS

pages 8-9: Seen here in 1959, near the end of its life, Chard Central (formerly Chard Joint) was built in 1866 to a design with a strong echo of Brunel. This small Somerset town once had three stations; now it has none.

pages 32-33: Prior to World War I, the extensive staff of an unknown LNWR station pose for the camera. Each man's status and position is defined by uniform. Notable is the range of ages represented.

pages 52-53: Seen here on a busy day soon before its closure, Wincanton was a typical small town station on the southern section of the Somerset & Dorset line. Nothing remains today.

pages 82-83 St Anne's Park, east of Bristol on the main line to Bath, was a classic country station, complete with signal box, siding, water tower and station house.

pages 144-145: Having come to the end of the line, a passenger seeks directions at Kyle of Lochalsh in the 1970s. The terminus of the line from Inverness is dramatically placed at the water's edge, with the Isle of Skye filling the horizon.

pages 176-177: This period 1950s scene at Castle Hedingham, in Essex, complete with J15 class locomotive and Scammell Mechanical Horse, was recreated in 2004 by the preserved Colne Valley Railway.

pages 202-203: This drawing by Claude Buckle of the famous Euston arch was included in a set of carriage prints of railway architecture, issued by the London Midland region of British Railways in the 1950s.

pages 212-213: In the 1940 evacuation of Dunkirk during World War II, the railways moved more than 300,000 troops away from South Coast ports. Here, French soldiers, safe on British soil, are directed to their train at Dover.

pages 226-227: The Meon Valley line has closed and the tracks have been removed, leaving only the buildings and the platforms. At Tisted, south of Alton, in 1957, decay is already taking hold.